Mark Waid, Al Ewing & Jim Zub
WRITERS

ISSUES #1-3, #7 & #9

Paco Medina
PENCILER

Juan Vlasco (#1-3) & **Paco Medina** (#7 & #9)
INKERS

Jesus Aburtov
COLOR ARTIST

ISSUES #4-6 & #10

Sean Izaakse
ARTIST

Marcio Menyz (#4-6 & #10), **Erick Arciniega** (#5, & #10) & **Jay David Ramos** (#6)
COLOR ARTISTS

ISSUE #8

Carlo Barberi
ARTIST

Jesus Aburtov
COLOR ARTIST

VC's Cory Petit
LETTERER

Yasmine Putri
COVER ART

Joshua James Shaw
NYX FAMILY DESIGNS

Alanna Smith
ASSOCIATE EDITOR

Tom Brevoort
EDITOR

FOR CONAN PROPERTIES INTERNATIONAL

Fred Malmberg
PRESIDENT

Jay Zetterberg
EXECUTIVE VICE PRESIDENT

Steve Booth
CHIEF OPERATIONS OFFICER

AVENGERS CREATED BY
Stan Lee & Jack Kirby

COLLECTION EDITOR: **Jennifer Grünwald**
ASSISTANT EDITOR: **Caitlin O'Connell**
ASSOCIATE MANAGING EDITOR: **Kateri Woody**
EDITOR, SPECIAL PROJECTS: **Mark D. Beazley**

VP PRODUCTION & SPECIAL PROJECTS: **Jeff Youngquist**
BOOK DESIGNER: **Adam Del Re**
SVP PRINT, SALES & MARKETING: **David Gabriel**
DIRECTOR, LICENSED PUBLISHING: **Sven Larsen**

EDITOR IN CHIEF: **C.B. Cebulski**
CHIEF CREATIVE OFFICER: **Joe Quesada**
PRESIDENT: **Dan Buckley**
EXECUTIVE PRODUCER: **Alan Fine**

AVENGERS: NO ROAD HOME. Contains material originally published in magazine form as AVENGERS NO ROAD HOME #1-10. First printing 2019. ISBN 978-1-302-91485-1. Published by MARVEL WORLDWIDE, INC., a subsidiary of MARVEL ENTERTAINMENT, LLC. OFFICE OF PUBLICATION: 135 West 50th Street, New York, NY 10020. **Printed in Canada.** DAN BUCKLEY, President, Marvel Entertainment; JOHN NEE, Publisher; JOE QUESADA, Chief Creative Officer; TOM BREVOORT, SVP of Publishing; DAVID BOGART, Associate Publisher & SVP of Talent Affairs; DAVID GABRIEL, SVP of Sales & Marketing, Publishing; JEFF YOUNGQUIST, VP of Production & Special Projects; DAN CARR, Executive Director of Publishing Technology; ALEX MORALES, Director of Publishing Operations; DAN EDINGTON, Managing Editor; SUSAN CRESPI, Production Manager; STAN LEE, Chairman Emeritus. For information regarding advertising in Marvel Comics or on Marvel.com, please contact Vit DeBellis, Custom Solutions & Integrated Advertising Manager, at vdebellis@marvel.com. For Marvel subscription inquiries, please call 888-511-5480. **Manufactured between 4/19/2019 and 5/21/2019 by SOLISCO PRINTERS, SCOTT, QC, CANADA.**

10 9 8 7 6 5 4 3 2 1

1

AVENGERS
NO ROAD HOME

Not long ago, the Earth was stolen to be used as a cosmic chess board by two cosmic entities, the Grandmaster and the Challenger. As the heroes of Earth fought to protect their planet from the warring factions, the Grandmaster introduced his daughter into the game disguised as a long-lost Avenger named Voyager.

But Voyager, inspired by the Avengers, turned on her father and aided in the Challenger's defeat. With Earth restored to its proper place in the universe, Voyager imprisoned the Challenger at the far reaches of the universe, hoping she could reform him.

For a while, Earth knew peace.

But something was stirring in the dark...

NEW YORK CITY.
WE ALL HAVE STORIES TO TELL.
73
THE AMPHISBAENA.
NOW THERE WAS A THREAT LIKE NO OTHER...
STORIES OF HEROISM.
STORIES OF HEARTBREAK.
"TITANIC IN STATURE, THE TWO-HEADED SERPENT BORN OF MEDUSA'S BROW COULD SWALLOW SWARMS OF MORTAL VILLAGERS WHOLE--AND DID--
"--UNTIL THE GODS OF OLYMPUS DESCENDED TO VANQUISH THE BEAST IN HARD-FOUGHT BATTLE!

"HERMES: MOST FLEET OF FOOT AND ALWAYS FIRST TO STRIKE.
"ARTEMIS: HER ARROWS, UNERRING AND DEADLY.
"POSEIDON: HIS TRIDENT CRASHING LIKE A TIDAL WAVE.
"ATHENA: A WARRIOR WOMAN LIKE NO OTHER.
"AND, OF COURSE, MY FATHER ZEUS, LORD OF SKY AND THUNDER AND KING OF THE GODS.
"NONE COULD STAND AGAINST US.

"OUR REVELRY WAS AS EPIC AS OUR VICTORY. NESTLED IN THE BOSOM OF THE COURTYARD OF OLYMPUS, OUR CHALICES KEPT BRIMMED BY DIONYSUS HIMSELF, WE CELEBRATED FOR DAYS.
"WE COULD SCARCE TEAR OURSELVES AWAY, AND WHY WOULD WE? THE MAJESTY OF OLYMPUS...THE GRANDEUR, THE BEAUTY...THERE IS NO PLACE ELSE SO MARVELOUS, SO WONDROUS AND RESPLENDENT IN ALL OF EXISTENCE THAN THE CRADLE OF THE IMMORTALS."
IT SIMPLY BEGGARS THE IMAGINATION.
THAT'S GREAT, MR. HERCULES. I CAN'T WAIT TO TELL MY KIDS. BUT, SEE, HERE'S THE THING...
POLICE DEPARTMENT CITY OF NEW YORK

...WE'RE KINDA IN THE MIDDLE OF A SITUATION HERE!
YES, YES, OF COURSE.
ALLOW ME TO ASSIST YOU!
HARDWARE TOOL & TOYS
SALE
POLICE
SWAT
HO, GOOD MAN, YOU MUST BE THE RANKING LEADER OF THIS GARRISON!
WHAT CAN YOU TELL ME ABOUT THE FOE IN YONDER TOOL FORTRESS?
THERE'S SOME KINDA FREAKY MONSTER IN THERE. PROBABLY ONE OF THOSE ALIEN TYPES.
NO ONE GOT A GOOD LOOK AT IT. ALL WE HEARD WAS CREEPY LAUGHTER AND THEN A BUNCHA LASERS SHOT UP TH--
HEY!
WHAT 'RE YOU DOIN'?!
POLI

HMMM--
ORGANIC THREAT DETECTED--
GUH!
RR!
BOOM
YOU FACE A WARRIOR OF SKILL SO GREAT THE BARDS HAVE RUN DRY THEIR QUILLS WHILE RECORDING MY D--
TRICKERY SHALL NOT SAVE YOU, BEAST!
ZANG ZANG ZANG ZANG ZANG

BACK OFF, BEARD-O!
COME ANY CLOSER AND I'LL POP PLASMA IN YOUR PIEHOLE!
ARE YOU SOME KIND OF... MILITARIZED DOG?
"DOG"?!
I'LL SHOW YOU A DOG, YOU MO--
ZAAAANG
CAREFUL NOW!
CREEEEEEEEEEEAAAAK
LOOK WHAT YOU DID...
UH-OH.

FEAR NOT, THE LION OF OLYMPUS REMAINS UNHARMED!
LEMME O, MUSCLE-BRAIN!
I WASN'T DOIN' NUTHIN' TA NO ONE!
YOU ATTACKED THE CITIZENS OF THIS FAIR CITY.
I TRIED TO SHOP AT THAT STORE AND THEY REFUSED TO SERVE ME! THEY JUST STARTED SCREAMIN' AN' FREAKIN' OUT!
SO, 'TWAS A MISUNDERSTANDING?
'TWAS! ONE HUNDRED PERCENT!
WHO ARE YOU?
THE NAME'S ROCKET.
AND WHAT IS THAT?
THIS?
THIS IS NUTHIN'.
ICE JOB, HERC! NOW PUT THE DOG DOWN AND WE'LL TAKE IT FROM HERE!
I AM NOT A DOG!
HOLD THERE, CONSTABULARY. I BELIEVE THERE HAS BEEN A MISTAKE.
TAKE THAT DOG &#$% BACK OR I'LL SHOVE THIS GRAVI-NADE UP YOUR STINKIN'--
EH?!
WHO TURNED OUT TH' LIGHTS?
THIS IS A STORY OF DARKNESS...
POLICE

...AND HOW TO HOLD IT BACK.
LOS ANGELES, CALIFORNIA. MOMENTS EARLIER.
Smith's DINER
OPEN
AND HOW'S YOUR MAN JERICHO?
WHO TOLD YOU ABOUT US?
JARVIS, MY AVENGERS GOSSIP MOLE.
HE IS NOT!
LEMME TELL YA, WANDA. TWO CUPS OF PG TIPS AND HIS MOUTH CAN'T STOP...

ANYWAY, WE'RE FINE.
THAT'S ACTUALLY WHY I'M ON THE WEST COAST, CLINT.
WE'RE LOOKING FOR A CONDO...

LIVING TOGETHER?
SO, IT'S GETTING SERIOUS...

IT'S...IT'S NICE.
I WANT TO SEE HOW IT FEELS TO SHARE LIVI SPACE. SEE WHETHER UNBALANCES THE EQUILIBRIUM BETWEEN US.

"SEEKING EQUILIBRIUM IN A SHARED LIVING SPACE. VOODOO POWERS A BIG PLUS."
SUCH A MOCKING TONE, CLINT...
I'M HAPPY FOR YOU, SERIOUSLY!
IN FACT, I WANT TO SEE MORE OF YOU AND THE GOOD DOCTOR.
I'M HELPING KATE AND HER REW RUN A NEW WEST COAST AVENGERS TEAM. I'M SURE YOU'VE SEEN OUR SOCIAL MEDIA BLITZ.
PIETRO IS TRYING TO BECOME AN INSTAGRAM STAR, SO I AVOID SOCIAL MEDIA THESE DAYS.
POINT IS, YOU AND JERICHO SHOULD JOIN US. I NEED A COUPLE VETERANS IN THE MIX TO SHOW THESE KIDS HOW IT'S DONE.
THANK YOU, BUT NO. I'VE HAD MY FAIR SHARE OF TEAM DRAMA FOR NOW.
HOWEVER, AS A CONCESSION, I BROUGHT YOU A PRESENT.
OH?
WHEN WE WERE BOXING UP SUPPLIES FROM AVENGERS MANSION, I CAME ACROSS SOME OF YOUR THINGS...
SMOKE RROW, PUTTY ARROW... CLASSIC!
SCARS AND STRIPES, AN UNAUTHORIZED CAPTAIN AMERICA BIOGRAPHY...OH, YEAH!
THAT WAS FROM WHEN CAP AND I HATED EACH OTHER'S GUTS AND I WAS LOOKING FOR DIRT TO USE AGAINST HIM...
AND THIS...

...A VIAL OF PYM PARTICLES FROM MY GOLIATH DAYS!
THAT SURE TAKES ME BACK...
SUPER-SOLDIERS, GENIUSES, GODS AND MUTANTS...I FELT LIKE THE LOW MAN ON EARTH'S MIGHTIEST TOTEM POLE.
WE ALL HAVE OUR MOMENTS OF DOUBT.
YEAH...
ANYTHING ELSE, OR SHOULD I BRING THE BILL?
NOTHING FOR ME, THANKS.
I'LL HAVE MORE COFFEE.
NO MILK, NO SUGAR.
Smith's
DINER
DARK AS DARK CAN BE.
UH...
THAT WASN'T ME.
I WANT TO HIDE FROM THE DARKNESS...TO WATCH FROM AFAR, TO LET THE STORY PLAY ITSELF OUT...

BUT THE AVENGERS TAUGHT ME BETTER THAN THAT.
WASHINGTON, D.C.
A PERFECT DAY.
WE GOT LUCKY, ALL RIGHT. NO CLOUDS MEANS ONE LESS THING TO CORRECT FOR IN THESE TESTS...
NOT QUITE WHAT I MEANT, SPECTRUM.
PLEASE, VISION--IT'S MONICA. WE'VE KNOWN EACH OTHER LONG ENOUGH.
HOW ARE THE READINGS ON YOUR END, HON?
GOOD NEWS AND BAD NEWS, I'M AFRAID.
KADESH BASE. IN THE MARIANA TRENCH.
I'LL LET DR. HO TAKE YOU THROUGH IT--SHE'S THE ROBOTICS SPECIALIST.
20.06
THANKS, BLUE MARVEL.
IT'S LIKE THIS--WHATEVER'S HAPPENING WITH THE VISION, THE REASON HIS SYSTEMS ARE DEGRADING LIKE THEY ARE--
I'M JUST GOING TO SAY IT: THE REASON HE'S DYING--

--WE WERE HOPING IT WAS A PROBLEM WITH HIS ENERGY INTAKE. IF IT WAS, WE'D HAVE A DIAGNOSIS.
BUT ACCORDING TO THESE READINGS, HE'S ABSORBING THE SUN'S RAYS AS WELL AS HE EVER DID. SO IT'S NOT HIS DIET.
BUT WHAT IT IS...WE STILL DON'T KNOW.
EXCEPT THAT IT STARTED AFTER THE HULK'S ATTACK.
DAMN. NOT SUCH A PERFECT DAY AFTER ALL--
ON THE CONTRARY, MONICA.
I DO NOT THINK OF THIS ONGOING PROCESS OF DETERIORATION AS MY DEATH-- BUT AS THE END OF MY LIFE.
TO LIVE-- TO BE TRULY HUMAN--I MUST ACCEPT THAT LIFE HAS AN END.
MY SYSTEMS ARE SLOWLY FAILING, AND I WILL SOON PASS AWAY. AND YET I HAVE THIS MOMENT.
I AM ALIVE.
I LIVE AND AM ALIVE.
IS THAT NOT PERFECT, EVEN THOUGH IT ENDS?
...
IAMBIC PENTAMETER?
I DABBLE. MY SON...HE ENJOYED SHAKESPEARE.
"OF ALL THE WONDERS THAT I YET HAVE HEARD, IT SEEMS TO ME MOST STRANGE THAT MEN SHOULD FEAR...

"...SEEING THAT DEATH, A NECESSARY END, WILL COME WHEN IT WILL COME."
JULIUS CAESAR.
MY BODY'S MADE OF ENERGY-- IN WHATEVER FORM I WANT THAT TO BE--
HMM. I'M NOT SURE HOW TO TAKE THAT, VISION.
--AND ENERGY CAN'T BE DESTROYED. I DON'T THINK I CAN DIE.
AM I LESS ALIVE? LESS HUMAN?
I COULDN'T SAY, MONICA.
I CAN ONLY ANSWER FOR MYSELF.
AHEM.
SPEAKING OF MONICA'S ABILITIES...
RIGHT--LET'S GET BACK TO IT. BY CHANGING INTO ELECTRICITY, I SHOULD BE ABLE TO WORK THROUGH YOUR SYSTEMS, VISION--
--CHECK FOR ANY FAULTS THAT AREN'T OBVIOUS FROM THE OUTSIDE.
LISTEN, LIKE ADAM SAID--THERE IS GOOD NEWS HERE.
NOW WE KNOW VISION CAN TAKE IN ALL THE ENERGY HE NEEDS TO FIGHT THIS THING, AND IT WON'T MAKE IT WORSE. SO AS LONG AS THE SUN DOESN'T SUDDENLY VANISH...
...
ME AND MY BIG MOUTH.
THEY TAUGHT ME TO FACE EVIL HEAD-ON. TO FIGHT TOGETHER...

...AGAINST WHAT CANNOT BE FOUGHT ALONE.
SOMEWHERE IN NEW MEXICO.
"...MMM-HMMM-MM... MM-MMM-MMM HMM...
"...I'D LIKE TO PRETEND THAT MY FATHER WAS WRONG...
"...BUT YOU DON'T WANT TO LIE...
"...NOT TO THE..."
I'M STIL THERE.

NEVER
LEFT!
GOD--
ERCIFUL
OD, HELP
ME--
I'M IN
HELL!
I'M
STILL IN
HELL!
I'M
STILL--
IN--
HHRRAAAARH!
SO WHAT
ELSE IS NEW,
BANNER?
I ASSEMBLED
THEM ONCE
BEFORE...
HULK?

...NOW I MUST DO SO AGAIN.
STARTING WITH THE STRONGEST.
I...DON'T KNOW IF YOU REMEMBER ME.
I AM VOYAGER. DAUGHTER OF EN DWI GAST--THE GRANDMASTER.
AND YOU... YOU ARE NEEDED.
I REMEMBER YOU.
DID YOU MAKE NIGHT FALL? THE ELDERS?
NO. BUT I SAW WHAT DID. AND I KNEW WE'D NEED HEROES.
WHAT DID THIS...IT'S THE MOST FRIGHTENING CREATURE I'VE EVER SEEN.
ALMOST.
HNH.
YOU SILVER-TONGUED DEVIL.
BUT STRENGTH ALONE CANNOT WIN. NOR WILL NUMBERS--THE ENEMY WILL SEE AN ARMY COMING.
AGAINST WHAT I SAW, WE NEED STRATEGY AND POWER.

FORTUNATELY, I KNOW AVENGERS WHO EMBODY BOTH.
CURIOUS. REVIEWING MY VISUAL MEMORY OF THE LAST FEW MOMENTS--THE SUN DID NOT SEEM TO SET. NIGHT SIMPLY...FELL.
BESIDES, ANY SUDDEN ROTATION OF THE EARTH WOULD HAVE LED TO SEVERE STRUCTURAL DAMAGE--
THIS ISN'T A STANDARD DAY/ NIGHT CYCLE, VISION--
--IT'S STILL NIGHT HERE IN THE PACIFIC OCEAN.
AND IN MOSCOW... BERLIN...LONDON, BEIJING, NEW YORK-- EVERYWHERE ON THE PLANET. AT ONCE.
HOW IS THAT POSSIBLE?
IT GETS WORSE, I'M AFRAID.
"THIS FACILITY HAS NEAR-INSTANT COMMUNICATION TH VARIOUS ALIEN WORLDS--
SOME KREE TRICK--
"--AND WHATEVER THIS IS--
ALL FIVE SUNS-- GONE!
IT'S-- IT'S THE END--
"--IT'S NOT LIMITED TO EARTH."
HHSSSS?

THERE'S A SHI'AR PLASMA-HARVESTING STATION IN THE HEART OF THEIR LOCAL SUN. NIGHT FELL THERE AS WELL.
MADNESS.
MONICA-- OUT OF US ALL, YOU HAVE PERHAPS THE MOST EXPERIENCE WITH THE INEXPLICABLE...
I'M NOT SURE, VISION. I'VE SEEN A LOT, BUT THIS...IT FEELS DIFFERENT. DARKER, SOMEHOW.
MAYBE IT'S TIME--
--TO ASSEMBLE--
VISION-- SPECTRUM--
--YOU ARE NEEDED.
MONICA? ARE YOU STILL THERE? VISION, RESPOND, PLEASE--
DAMMIT-- THE COMM STREAM'S CUT OUT SOMEHOW--
WELL, AT LEAST THEY CAN TAKE CARE OF THEMSELVES, DR. BRASHEAR.
RIGHT NOW, I'M MORE WORRIED ABOUT THOSE WHO CAN'T...
TRUE-- UNIVERSAL NIGHTFALL MEANS UNIVERSAL PANIC. LIVES ARE IN DANGER EVERYWHERE-- LITERALLY.
WE'RE GOING TO BE BUSY...

OKAY--LET'S NOT PANIC HERE, PEOPLE.
PRETTY SURE THIS IS A ROUTINE SUN OUTAGE, AND YOUR FRIENDLY NEIGHBORHOOD AVENGERS ARE ON THE CASE.
SO THERE'S NO REASON TO BE SCARED--
YEAH? WHAT ABOUT THAT, DUDE?
...WHAT?

OH, THAT.
SCARLET WITCH--YOU ARE NEEDED.
YOU CAN DEFY REALITY ITSELF WITH YOUR MAGIC--IF WE'RE TO FIGHT THIS ENDLESS NIGHT, WE'LL NEED YOUR ABILITIES.

THERE'S REALLY NO CHOICE, IS THERE?
GUESS NOT. AVENGERS ASSEMBLE, RIGHT?
IN FACT, SPEAKING OF WEST COAST AVENGERS, I CAN MAKE SOME CALLS--
BARTON--GET LOST. THIS IS SERIOUS.
WE DON'T NEED THE ARROW GUY.
WHAT?

HULK, IF THIS IS ABOUT ME SHOOTING YOU-- ME AND BRUCE SETTLED THAT--
DID YOU.
BANNER COMES TO YOU TO HELP KILL ME--KILL US. AND INSTEAD OF SENDING HIM TO A SHRINK... YOU GO ALONG WITH IT.
YOU PUT AN ARROW IN OUR HEAD.
AND NOW YOU THINK IT'S SETTLED.
YOU KNOW WHAT? TAG ALONG, BARTON. MAKE YOURSELF-- HNH--USEFUL.
JUST DON'T FIND YOURSELF ALONE WITH ME. EVER.
Y-YEAH? OR WHAT?

OR I'LL SETTLE IT.
I WONDER IF CONTACTING THE HULK WAS A MISTAKE. IF HE TURNS ON US, I'M NOT SURE ANYONE HERE HAS THE STRENGTH TO STOP HIM.
BUT THERE IS ONE WHO MIGHT--PERHAPS. I WAS HOPING TO BUILD OUR FORCES FURTHER BEFORE I SPOKE TO HIM.

.BUT NOW AS GOOD A ME AS ANY.
RTAL AT 'CLOCK!
VOYAGER!
HERCULES, YOU ARE NEEDED!
LY CRAP, AT'S THE HULK!
EVERYONE STEP AWAY WITH YOUR HANDS UP!
STAND DOWN, SIR. DO YOU NOT SEE THAT THIS IS AN ASSEMBLY OF HEROES?
ONLY THING THESE GOONS UNDERSTAND IS A SUPERIOR FIREPOWER.
HEY, HULK.
DON'T HAVE TIME NEGOTIATE WITH LOCAL LAW ENFORCEMENT.
I UNDERSTAND, MILADY. GIVE ME JUST A MOMENT...
ROCKET.
LONG TIME, HUH?

THE HULK **BLEW UP** A WHOLE TOWN IN **IOWA**--
THAT'S HOW THEY'RE SELLING THAT?
THIS **POSTURING** SERVES **NO ONE**. MY FRIENDS AND I ARE ABOUT TO EMBARK ON A **QUEST**.

YOU CAN'T JUST UP AND LEAVE AFTER THE **DESTRUCTION** YOU CAUSED!

AMENDS WILL BE MADE, BUT NOT RIGHT **NOW**!
IF YOU CONTACT **TONY STARK**, HE'LL SEE THAT THIS IS PROPERLY DEALT WITH.
WELL, **HELLO** THERE, METAL MAN...

CAN I HELP YOU?
STAND STILL FOR A SEC, OKAY? JUST WANNA GET A SMALL PIECE O--

I HAVE NO COMPONENTS I CAN SPARE.
EXCUSE MY LACK OF DENSITY, BUT I AM MONITORING A **SIGNIFICANT** POTENTIAL **THREAT**.
WHAT TH--?!

WHAT'S HE STARIN' AT?
EVERY MOMENT WE WAIT, THE SITUATION WORSENS. COME WITH US NOW.
OF COURSE! A HERO SUMMONED ALWAYS ANSWERS THE CALL!
WHERE ARE WE GOING?
SWAT
YOUR ME. MOUNT OLYMPUS.
THERE'S BEEN AN ATTACK--
OLYMPUS?!
TAKE ME THERE, WOMAN! DO IT NOW!
I WILL, BUT MORE ALLIES ARE NEEDED BEFORE WE AN--
NAY! YOU SAID EVERY MOMENT BRINGS MORE CALAMITY.
OPEN THE DAMNED PORTAL!
VERY WELL.
U CRAZY DS HAVE N, 'CAUSE 'M OUT!
HEY!
NO FAI--
"BUT HERCULES..."

...BRACE YOURSELF!

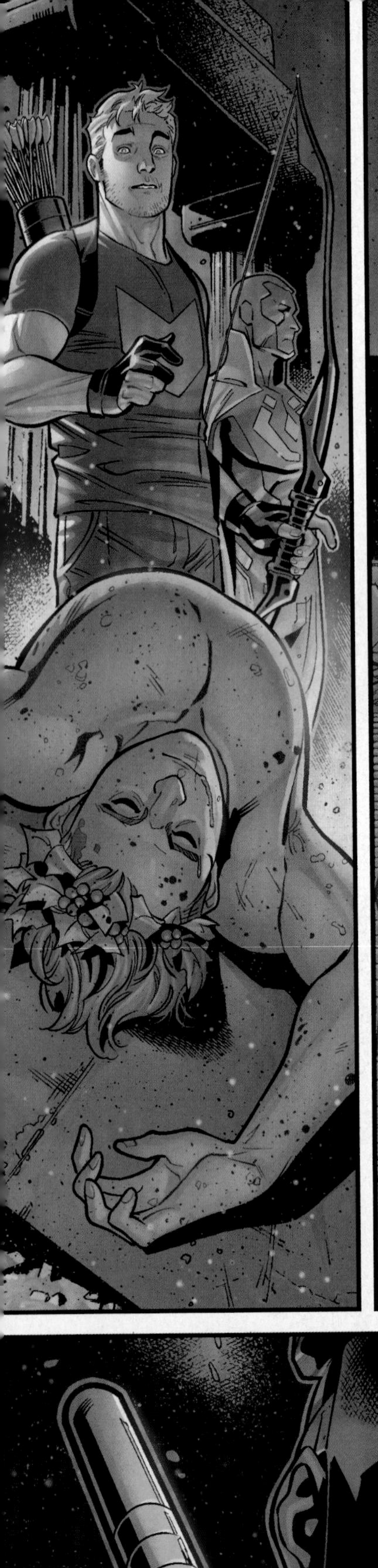

MY GODS.

I SAW DARKNESS.

THE AIR SMELLS OF BURNING FLESH AND SMOLDERING METAL.
IT TASTES OF IMPOSSIBILITY. SOMEONE HAS SLAIN THE IMMORTALS.
IN AGES PAST, THEY WERE WORSHIPED.
OW THEY WILL E MOURNED.
BEFORE ANYONE COULD STOP IT, THE GODS OF OLYMPUS WERE SLAIN.
WE WILL FIND WHOEVER DID THIS TO YOUR PEOPLE--
MY FRIEND, YOU HAVE OUR CONDOLENCES.
YOU.
WHAT HAPPENED HERE? YOU MUST HAVE SEEN!
HOW DID YOU KNOW TO BRING US?
I--
BR...
...BROTHER...?

I'D GROWN ACCUSTOMED TO WATCHING THE DRAMA UNFOLD FROM MY PLACE UPON THE FAR SHORE.
NOW, SEEING IT *FIRSTHAND*...
SISTER ATHENA!
VISION! WANDA! BRING AID!
SISTER, IT WILL BE ALL RIGHT! WE'LL *SAVE* YOU--
YOU ARE...TOO LATE. THE LIGHT...
...SHE TOOK THE LIGHT FROM US...
WHO? WHO DID THIS?
THE QUEEN... THE QUEEN OF *NIGHT*...
YOU MEAN--
DO *NOT*...
KOFF
...YOU *KNOW*...T YOU MU *NEVER* SA *NAME*.
THIS IS *MY FAULT!* I SHOULD HAVE *BEEN* HERE--DEFENDING MY *HOME*--
THERE...YOU ARE. ALWAYS TRYING TO CLAIM... *BOTH* OLYMPUS AND...THE EARTH...
BROTHER, BORN OF GOD *AND* MORTAL... YOU NEVER TRULY *WERE*...ONE OF *US*.
THAT'S NOT *TRUE!*
SOME CALLED US BEINGS OF *MYTH*... BUT TRUE MYTHS HAVE...A *FINAL CHAPTER*.
THE DAY... THAT *YOUR* LEGEND...REACHES ITS END AS WELL...
...ONLY THEN WILL YOU...FINALLY BE...
...BE *HOME*...

AND THEN, SHE IS GONE.
MY HEART BREAKS WITH HIS.
SO...
...THIS "QUEEN OF NIGHT"...?
IN THE ANCIENT GREEK MYTHS, THE GODDESS OF NIGHT WAS A WOMAN NAMED NYX, YES?
BEFORE I CAN RAISE THE ALARM...I SENSE IT. SOMETHING STIRRING IN THE NIGHT AIR.
AYE. AND IF MY FATHER'S STORIES OF HER ARE TRUE, SHE... SHE MAY WELL POSSESS ENOUGH POWER TO HAVE DONE THIS.
IF SO, WHERE IS SHE NOW? VOYAGER, WHAT KNOWLEDGE CAN YOU PASS TO--
NO!
E DARKNESS
AS COME TO
CLAIM US...

...AND THERE IS NO ESCAPE.
YOUR SISTER WAS RIGHT, SON OF ZEUS.
SHE SHOULD NOT HAVE SAID MY NAME.

come back, True Believers, to THE ASSEMBLY! If you were around for AVENGERS: NO SURRENDER, you w this is the part where we regale you with behind-the-scenes tales of making this crazy contraption we ll a weekly comic. If you weren't around, stick to this page like glue--we're gonna bring you up to speed!

er the success of AVENGERS: NO SURRENDER, the bigwigs at Marvel had one question: Can you do i in? The answer wasn't that we could, but that we wanted to. Putting out a weekly book is an exhausting rn like nothing else--but with the team we had, and the characters we got to play with, and how weird we e allowed to get (hey, remember that time a poker game saved the world?), it was also about as delightfu as making comics can be. So we got the gang back together, and boy did they deliver!

ll have plenty more stories in the weeks to come about that whole process, but for now, let's get caugh up with our colorful cast!

HERCULES: Not long ago, the Prince of Power tired of his role as a boisterous embarrassment to the Avengers and began to turn his life around. He got sober, rejoined the Avengers, and played a major role in saving Earth from the Challenger and the Grandmaster. But his team disbanded after that event, as did the other teams involved and he's been on his own since.

CKET RACCOON: Rocket's life was recently rocked by tragedy. The Guardians of Galaxy, the closest people he has to family, have more or less disbanded, leaving cket to his own devices. Which is never a good idea. *[This story takes place before ARDIANS OF THE GALAXY #1]*

HAWKEYE: Clint Barton killed Bruce Banner (at Bruce's own request) to prevent him from becoming the monstrous Hulk seen in an apocalyptic vision of the future, but it didn't take He and his teammate, Red Wolf, served a pivotal role in defeating the Grandmaster and the Challenger before going their separate ways. Currently, he moonlights as a mentor to the newly formed West Coast Avengers.

ARLET WITCH: Wanda Maximoff was recently reunited with her brother Pietro, after the battle n the Grandmaster and the Challenger left him locked out of time. Their relationship is stronger n ever, and with Doctor Voodoo as her partner in love and magic, Wanda is finally finding some asure of stability in her life. What could go wrong?

SPECTRUM: Monica Rambeau can turn into any form of light, making her one of the mos powerful beings in existence. It also means that--like her partner, the Blue Marvel--she's unlikely to age...or die. She has a long history with the Avengers, and most recently worked with the Ultimates to solve problems on a cosmic scale.

E HULK: Bruce Banner died when Clint Barton shot him in the head with a gamma ow...or so he thought. When the Challenger reawakened the Hulk to use as a pawn in grudge match against the Grandmaster, Bruce had a horrible realization: he couldn't Now he roams the backroads of America, looking for wrongs to right...as something k grows inside of him...

VISION: When the Challenger deployed the Hulk, Vision was the Avengers' first line of defense, and he paid dearly for it. Hulk shattered his solar gem and damaged his synthezoid body irreparably. Toni Ho has been trying to stop the gradual corruption of Vision's systems, but Vision is becoming convinced that the only way he can truly experience mortality...is to let himself expire.

YAGER: Va Nee Gast appeared at Earth's darkest moment in the guise of Valerie Vector, ng-lost founding Avenger with the power to teleport. She was later revealed to be the ndmaster's daughter, but the heroism of the Avengers rubbed off on her, and she helped m save the planet. Once the Challenger was defeated, she took him to the edge of space, ing to help him see the light as she had.

re, you're up to speed--just in time for us to blow it all up! If there's something you'd like us to cover in iture Assembly, email us at MHEROES@MARVEL.COM with your message marked "Okay to Print"--you might just learn something new!

d if you haven't read AVENGERS: NO SURRENDER, be sure to snag the collection! If it's as fun to read as it was to work on, you're guaranteed to have a blast!

2

METIMES, PEOPLE ASK
E, "HAWKEYE, HOW DO
OU DO WHAT YOU DO?
"ARE YOU JUST LUCKY, OR WHAT?"
HRRH. I... STILL DON'T FULLY UNDERSTAND THIS, VA NEE GAST.
WHAT MAKES THESE AVENGERS FIGHT LIKE THAT? AGAINST GODS AND GOD KILLERS?
HE FAR SHORE.
HALLENGER'S PRISON AT
HE EDGE OF EVERYTHING.
OT LONG AGO.
EY'RE JUST... MORTAL.
WHAT DRIVES THEM ON? WHAT COULD POSSIBLY--
HRRRH!
NNNHH--
BUT IT NEVER LASTS.
ACTUALLY, THERE'S A PRETTY SIMPLE SECRET.
WHAT WAS THAT? THAT... BURST OF AGONY...
I FELT IT TOO, CHALLENGER. LIKE SOMETHING TEARING THE SKIN OF THE UNIVERSE...
SEE, IN THIS WORLD, ONE MINUTE EVERYTHING'S OKAY-- OR NOT OKAY, BUT PREDICTABLE.

HERE.
MOUNT OLYMPUS.
IMMORTALS AT PLAY...
A NOSTALGIC SIGHT, BUT--
SHH.
WATCH.
KROOM
YOUR LUCK RUNS OUT.
GODS OF OLYMPUS.
DO YOU REMEMBER MY NAME?
AND THERE'S NEVER ANY WARNING.

AND SUDDENLY, IT'S ALL ON *YOU.*
IT CANNOT BE...
HERMES! *UN,* BOY! FIND *ERCULES*--TELL *M THE QUEEN OF NIGHT IS RETURNED!*
I DO YOUR *BIDDING,* FATHER--
AS I, *HYPNOS,* MUST DO MY *MOTHER'S* BIDDING.
GO TO *SLEEP,* MY FRIEND.
IT'LL GO *EASIER* THAT WAY.
TO FIGHT GODS AND GOD KILLERS.
TO FIGHT A WHOLE *WORLD* THAT WANTS TO *CRUSH* YOU AND CRUSH YOUR *FRIENDS.*

YOU LOCKED ME AWAY, LORD ZEUS.
SENT ME TO ROT UNTIL THE SUN WAS PARTED FROM THE EARTH.
BUT THEN THE SUN WAS TORN FROM THE SKY. I AM FREE--FREE TO SEE WHAT YOU'VE ALL BEEN DOING.
AND WHAT DO I FIND?
NO--TOO FAST--
FATHER! FATHER, HELP US!
YOUR ONLY EPICS ARE PAST GLORIES. YOUR ONCE-GREAT POETRY IS NOW MERE BANTER.
YOU ARE UNWORSHIPED... UNCARING...
MURDERERS! I'LL DESTROY YOU FOR--
--HURRKK--
...TOO WEAK TO RESIST THE TRUE DEATH.
AND YOU'VE ONLY GOT WHAT'S IN YOUR HANDS.
NO!
YOU--YOU WILL DIE FOR THIS! YOU!
FOUL DEMON OF THE DARK--

A BOW AND
RROW AGAINST
HE LIGHTNING.
DEMON?
I GAVE YOU ALL I HAD. I GAVE YOU THE UNKNOWN AND THE UNKNOWABLE.
I GAVE YOU THE NIGHT--
HHKK--
--AND YOU WASTED IT.
SO HOW DO YOU DO IT?
SHE'S KILLING THEM ALL--
REVENGE. A MOTIVE I UNDERSTAND.
SHE WON'T BE STOPPED UNTIL SOMEONE STOPS HER...
I--I CAN'T LEAVE. I HAVE A RESPONSIBILITY.
SOMEONE HAS TO GUARD YOU--
HRRRH. BUT CAN YOU STAY, VA NEE GAST?
WHEN DID THE EARTH PART FROM THE SUN?
WAS IT WHEN WE MOVED IT? FOR OUR GAME?
"DID YOU FREE HER?"
DESPAIR
DESPAIR
OH...OH, THIS GRIEF... MY HEART...
HUSH. YOU ARE TOUCHED BY OIZYS NOW--MY MOST FAVORED OFFSPRING.
OIZYS IS MISERY.

HOW DO YOU FIGHT WHEN THERE'S NO HOPE?
TELL ME. WHEN YOU CAST ME DOWN AND TOOK THE NIGHT SHARDS WITHIN MY SOUL...
...WHAT DID YOU DO WITH THEM?
I...I PLACED ONE WITH AN ALLY IN A PLACE OF KNOWLEDGE...
...ONE WITH AN ENEMY... IN A PLACE OF DREAMS...
...AND ONE...
DESPAIR
DESPAIR
...ONE IN A FAR-OFF PARADISE...
N-NO! NO, I AM ZEUS! I HOLD THE LIGHTNING IN MY HAND! YOU'LL LEARN NO MORE!
I SEE.
AND--AND WHEN MY SON LEARNS OF THIS--HE WILL BRING THE FORCES OF THE AGE UPON YOUR HEAD!
I HAVE FELT THE POWER OF THE NEW HEROES! THE AVENGERS OF THE WRONGED!
THEY ARE TRULY EARTH'S MIGHTIEST--AND YOU WILL NEVER--
THE LIGHT IS YOURS NO LONGER.
YOU WILL NOT BE MISSED.
KRAKK
HOW DO YOU FIGHT THE EN OF THE WORLD

HOW DO YOU DO WHAT I DO?
THE GODS ARE DEAD. BUT THERE IS MORE YET TO BE DONE. THIS UNIVERSE... IS SPOILED.
ONCE I REGAIN THE SHARDS OF MY MISSING POWER, I CAN WIPE IT CLEAN AND START A BETTER ONE. BUT FOR NOW...
WELL... HERE'S MY SECRET.
NOW I CLAIM YOUR THRONE, MIGHTY ZEUS.
AND THE BARE BEGINNINGS OF MY FULL POWER.
THE DAY OF THE GODS IS DONE.
LET FALL THE NIGHT.
I HAVE NO IDEA.
I MEAN, THERE'S GOTTA BE SOMETHING TO IT. CAN'T BE JUST LUCK.
SHE WON'T BE STOPPED.
THERE'S NO CHOICE, IS THERE?
NO.
YOU CAN'T FIGHT IT ALONE, EITHER.
ALL I KNOW IS, IF I STOPPED TO THINK ABOUT IT...
GO. ASSEMBLE YOUR AVENGERS, VOYAGER.
I LOOK FORWARD TO YOUR RETURN.
HRRRH.
...I'D NEVER GET ANYTHING DONE.

NOW.
SO I ACT WITHOUT THINKING. EVERYBODY KNOWS THAT.
"THE AVENGERS OF THE WRONGED."
FRANKLY, I EXPECTED MORE.
LIKE WHEN I SEE THIS CRAZY GOD-KILLING CHICK PUT HER CLAWS THROUGH WANDA'S HEAD...
...THERE'S NO TIME FOR HESITATION.
THIS ISN'T A CAREFULLY CONSIDERED ACTION.
IT'S ALL ABOUT INSTINCT.

BOOM
RRRR--!
BOOM
YUP, THAT'S THE CLINT BARTON WAY--"SHOOT FIRST, GET SCARED LATER."
BOOM
YOU!!!
YOU WILL PAY WITH BLOOD FOR WHAT YOU'VE DONE!
SCRATCH THAT.
WATCHING HER DODGE GOD FISTS AND LASER BEAMS WITHOUT BREAKING A SWEAT...
...I'M A BIT FREAKED OUT NOW.
GOTTA SLOW MY BREATHING.
GOTTA KEEP MY HEAD IN THE GAME.
DON'T SHOOT AT HER...
...SHOOT WHERE SHE'S GONNA END UP.
BOOM

YOUR FATHER SPOKE OF YOUR PROWESS, HERACLES THE HALF-BREED.
WHY DON'T YOU SHOW ME?
I'LL WIPE THAT SMILE FROM YOUR LIPS, WENCH!
HUSH.
SLASH
GRAAH!
MY SOUL WAS BROKEN INTO SHARDS AND SCATTERED ACROSS THE UNIVERSE--DID YOU KNOW THAT? I AM AT MY WEAKEST.
I THOUGHT THAT MIGHT AT LEAST MAKE THIS ENTERTAINING.
APPARENTLY NOT--
UHHH!

NICE WORK, BIG GREEN!
NOW HOLD HER STEADY!
HNH?!
FWSSSH
ZEEEE
EEEEEN
OWW!
I AM DARKNESS ITSELF, YOU FOOL. I CANNOT BE HELD.
RIIP
GRAAH
SHE'S TOYING WITH US, LIKE IT'S ALL A GAME.
C-CLINT?
I'M HERE, WANDA. JUST HOLD ON...

IS THAT ALL?
I WAS TOLD THE FORCES OF THE AGE WOULD COME TO THWART ME. I EXPECTED HEROES.
I COULD HAVE LEFT THIS BATTLE TO MY CHILDREN...
WE'LL BRING YOU TO JUSTICE FOR WHAT YOU'VE DONE!
KRAK
UNNH!
WILL YOU NOW?
SLASH
AHHH!
VIZ, IF YOU AND I STRIKE SIMULTANEOUSLY, WE MIGHT BE ABLE TO GIVE HERC ENOUGH TIME TO HIT HER HARD.
AGREED, SPECTRUM--BUT WE MUST TIME IT PERFECTLY. STAY HIDDEN WITHIN MY CIRCUITRY UNTIL I GIVE THE SIGNAL.
SHE'S TROUNCING MYTHS, MONSTERS AND COSMIC ELDERS LIKE THEY'RE NOTHING.
IF SHE GETS AHOLD OF ME...
WHEN SHE GETS AHOLD OF ME...
DON'T THINK ABOUT IT.

IF I THINK ABOUT IT... I WON'T...
I CAN'T...
YOUR SKILLS ARE **WORTHLESS** HERE...
...AS IS YOUR **COURAGE.**
WORTHLESS
ORTHLESS
WHAT GOOD AM I?
I DON'T WANT TO DIE HERE...
A COCKY GUY WITH A *BOW...*
...WHAT CHANCE HAVE I GOT?
NO CHANCE.
NO CHANCE AT ***ALL.***
AT ALL
AT ALL

SPECTRUM--

--NOW!

AHHHH--!
TO HELLS WITH YOU ALL...
SHOW US THE WAY--
--AND I'LL GLADLY FOLLOW!
THOOM
THERE NOW!
FINALLY A WORTHY BLOW FROM THE SON OF ZEUS!
COME. DEFEND THE GRAVES OF YOUR FAMILY...
NO! IF SHE'S GOADING US-- THIS IS ALL A DISTRACTION!
IF HER CHILDREN AREN'T HERE, SHE MUST HAVE SENT THEM TO RETRIEVE THE SHARDS OF HER SOUL!
NOW THAT I SEE HER POW I CAN SENSE T LOCATION.
WE MUS INTERC THEM.

NO!
I WILL SLAY NYX HERE AND N--
ENOUGH WITH THE PORTAL POPPIN'!
OH GREAT, NOW WHERE ARE WE--
HMMM--
VOYAGER, Y--
GO!
YOUR POWER...
...IT INTRIGUES ME!
NNNG--!
YOU'RE A FINDER, AREN'T YOU?
YOU LOCATE AND TRANSPORT...
HOW...
...USEFUL.
HEEEE HEEE HEE--

WH...WHERE...?
HOSPITAL BED...? HOW'D I GET...
WANDA!
VISION! ANYBODY! IS ANYBODY THERE?
HELLO?

DON'T PANIC. BREATHE. PUT IT TOGETHER.
YOU'RE IN A HOSPITAL, WHICH IS FRANKLY NOT SURPRISING GIVEN THAT THE LAST THING YOU REMEMBER IS SHOOTING STICKS AT A GOD.
AND YET, YOU CLEARLY LIVED TO TELL THE TALE. AGAIN.
CLINT BARTON, PROFESSIONAL WEEBLE. HE WOBBLES, BUT HE WON'T FALL DOWN.
72
98
19
84
95
THERE HAD TO HAVE BEEN ANOTHER BATTLE. SOMEONE BROUGHT YOU HERE FOR SOME REASON. BUT WHATEVER HAPPENED, YOU SEEM TO BE ALL RIGHT.
JUST THE USUAL POST-SLOBBERKNOCKER ACHES AND PAINS, YEAH?

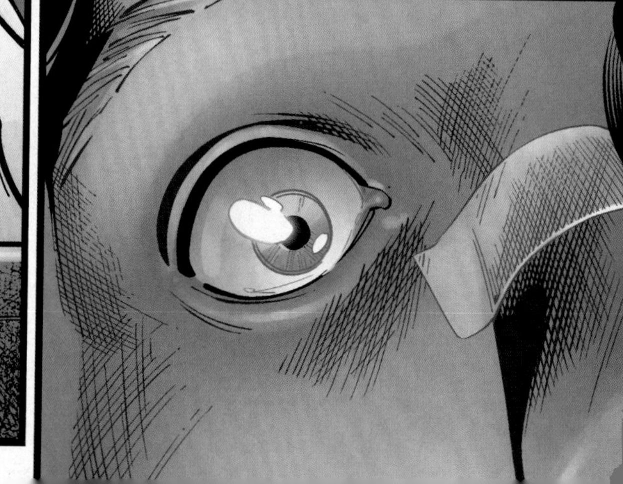

72
98
84
95
140
60
44
80

HELLO? NURSE?
DOCTOR?
CAN ANYBODY HEAR ME?
...
WHAT DID YOU EXPECT, YOU OVERDUE IDIOT?
LOOK AT WHO YOU ARE. LOOK AT WHERE YOU'VE *BEEN.*

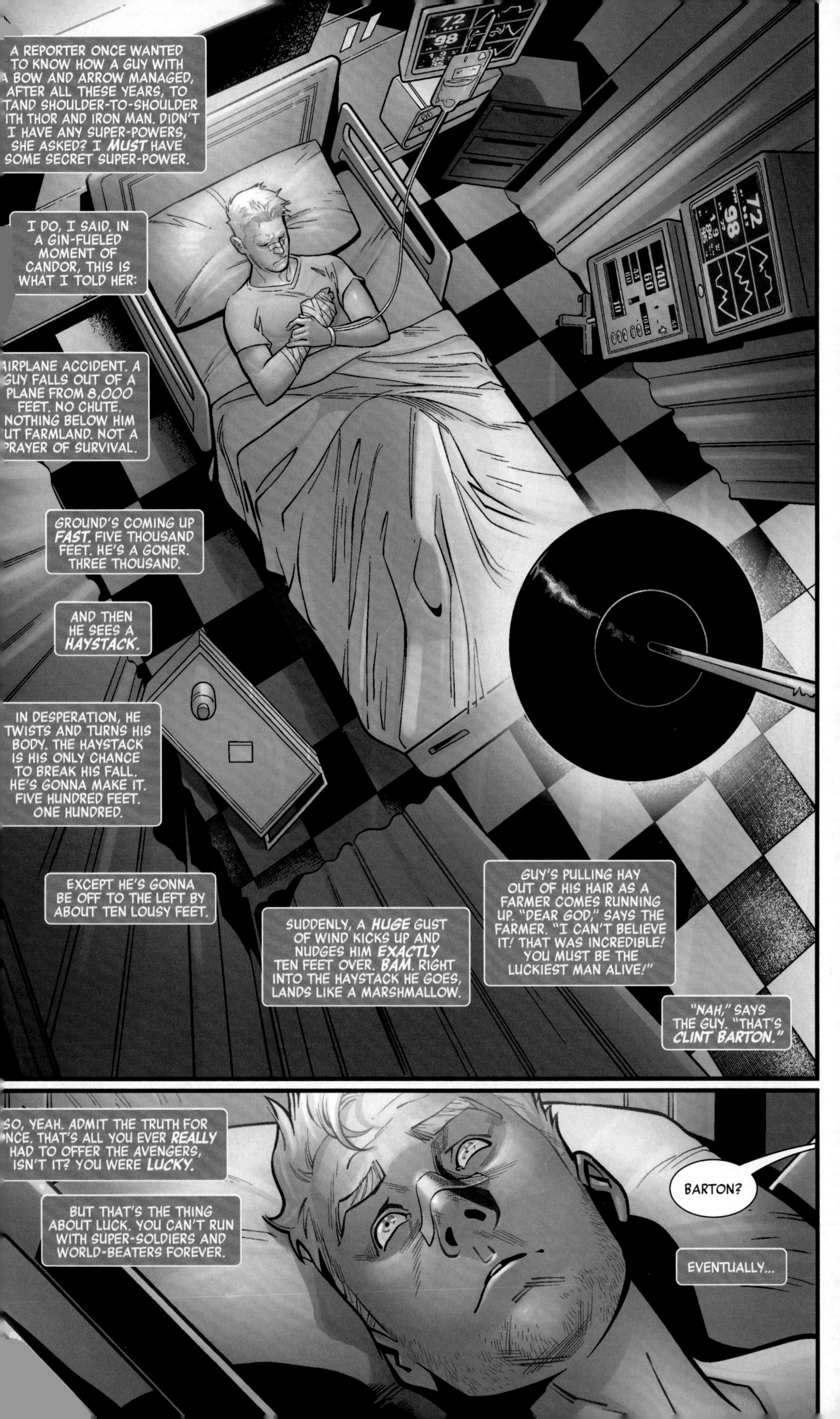

A REPORTER ONCE WANTED TO KNOW HOW A GUY WITH A BOW AND ARROW MANAGED, AFTER ALL THESE YEARS, TO TAND SHOULDER-TO-SHOULDER ITH THOR AND IRON MAN. DIDN'T I HAVE ANY SUPER-POWERS, SHE ASKED? I MUST HAVE SOME SECRET SUPER-POWER.
I DO, I SAID. IN A GIN-FUELED MOMENT OF CANDOR, THIS IS WHAT I TOLD HER:
AIRPLANE ACCIDENT. A GUY FALLS OUT OF A PLANE FROM 8,000 FEET. NO CHUTE. NOTHING BELOW HIM UT FARMLAND. NOT A RAYER OF SURVIVAL.
GROUND'S COMING UP FAST. FIVE THOUSAND FEET. HE'S A GONER. THREE THOUSAND.
AND THEN HE SEES A HAYSTACK.
IN DESPERATION, HE TWISTS AND TURNS HIS BODY. THE HAYSTACK IS HIS ONLY CHANCE TO BREAK HIS FALL. HE'S GONNA MAKE IT. FIVE HUNDRED FEET. ONE HUNDRED.
EXCEPT HE'S GONNA BE OFF TO THE LEFT BY ABOUT TEN LOUSY FEET.
SUDDENLY, A HUGE GUST OF WIND KICKS UP AND NUDGES HIM EXACTLY TEN FEET OVER. BAM. RIGHT INTO THE HAYSTACK HE GOES, LANDS LIKE A MARSHMALLOW.
GUY'S PULLING HAY OUT OF HIS HAIR AS A FARMER COMES RUNNING UP. "DEAR GOD," SAYS THE FARMER. "I CAN'T BELIEVE IT! THAT WAS INCREDIBLE! YOU MUST BE THE LUCKIEST MAN ALIVE!"
"NAH," SAYS THE GUY. "THAT'S CLINT BARTON."
SO, YEAH. ADMIT THE TRUTH FOR NCE. THAT'S ALL YOU EVER REALLY HAD TO OFFER THE AVENGERS, ISN'T IT? YOU WERE LUCKY.
BUT THAT'S THE THING ABOUT LUCK. YOU CAN'T RUN WITH SUPER-SOLDIERS AND WORLD-BEATERS FOREVER.
BARTON?
EVENTUALLY...

...YOUR LUCK RUNS OUT.
GUESS WHAT, BARTON?
YOU'RE ALONE.
TIME TO SETTLE UP.
AND THERE'S NEVER ANY WARNING.
SO TRY NOT TO THINK ABOUT IT.

come back to the Assembly, True Believers! You've just been introduced to the Marvel U's newest Big Bads--Nyx and he some family! Wondering why these wicked world conquerors look so rad? It's because Joshua James Shaw, the creative ctor at Marvel TV and the genius behind Doctor Strange's recent redesign, is the one who designed them for us! You car ck out his final design sheet below, along with the original descriptions sent over to him by our wonderful writing team

Designs by Joshua James Shaw

THE TWINS--APATE (Deceit) and DOLOS (Trickery): One is the deceiver and one is the believer-- one represents malevolent lies and one represents ignorant lies. Apate is a wiry woman with a piercing ze who never smiles. She sees hate in everyone and brings it out of them. She has short hair and a rec ecorative marking beneath both her eyes. Her clothing is short and simple, so she can easily move anc aneuver in combat. She has a dusky red half-cloak that covers her arms most of the time, and when he nds/arms do emerge from beneath, they're almost always wielding a thin and deadly dagger. If she throws t both her hands at the same time from beneath the cloak, a dozen or more of these daggers may spray ou a torrent of death. If she can embed one of these daggers in a being's back, she can drive them into furious ger and send them to attack targets of her choice.

olos is a wiry man, Apate's twin. He has an equally piercing gaze but always with a wicked smile or s face. He's constantly delighted with his own cleverness. He also has short hair, and beneath his eyes e blue decorative markings. His clothing is a mirror image of his sister's in terms of style and cut, bu s half-cloak (hanging off the opposite shoulder) is dusky blue. When his hands emerge from beneath he ually has a luminescent blue sand-like substance in his hands. This powder can be used to create clouds shimmering blue fog that's hard to see through or, when struck in the eyes with it, it can overwhelm a erson's senses so they can't tell what's real and what's an illusion.

NYX (Night): The Mother of Night is almost vampiric in appearance, with albino, marble-like white in set against a thick black hooded cloak that seems to meld with her impossibly black hair. Her nails, nds and forearms are black, speckled with stars (stars in the sky, not five-pointed icons of stars) that get ore numerous and dense until the white skin resumes by the elbow. Nyx's eyes are solid black glistening arbles, with no pupils.

HYPNOS (Sleep): Hypnos is noble, upstanding, a general-type. He's also an ends-justify-the-means pe--he'll willingly follow his mother in whatever she wants to do and believe it's right because she saic He's also the sleep of reason--the sleep people are in before they get "woke" to the reality of things. He ows he's good, therefore what he does is good and his family is also good. He's unquestioning. Hypnos pears to be a strong Greek warlord, but his armor is black sections rimmed with silver accents insteac the red and gold or earth tones we'd expect. His helm has an ornate cover over his eyes so we canno e them (and we never will), making his mouth a bit more creepy. He wields a pair of classic Xiphos-style ecian blades that not only cut their opponent but also sap their strength and clarity.

OIZYS (Misery): Just this horrible, oozing mind-creature, almost Cthulhu-esque, hard to look at. She's the voice ne head--we all know it--the inner demon that wants you to suffer. She can infect people and take them over, leave n not in their right mind. In terms of physicality, she is a scrawny, serpentine, alien figure that squats on Nyx's ulder or coils around the throats of the people she's influencing. (When given power by her mother, she gets bigger meaner.) Extremely bony hands/fingers and a lower body that's more wormlike than human. She has no eyes, just shy bumps where they should be and a huge mouth filled with tiny jagged, stained teeth. Her body and head are pped in shredded and soiled rags. Even in the midst of a pitched battle with a cacophony of noise, her psychic ispers" can cut through the din and build up dread and doubt within her victims if they're not on their guard.

3

When Rocket woke up, he was being born again.
It hurt like Hell.
Maybe it was Hell.

The pain was an old song, played from memory. Played loud.
A symphony of déjà vu with a chorus of razors.

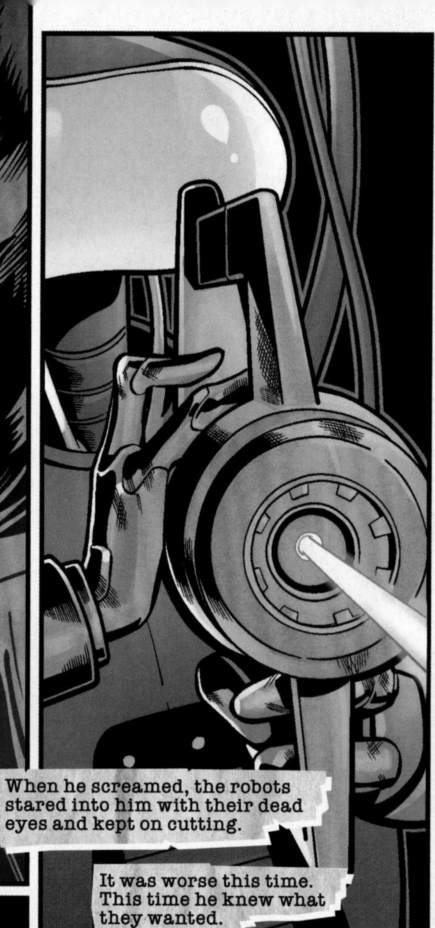
When he screamed, the robots stared into him with their dead eyes and kept on cutting.
It was worse this time. This time he knew what they wanted.

They wanted something that could take their place. Do the job they were bored with.
They wanted to mutate a therapy animal into a warden for a cosmic asylum. Into a **Ranger.**

"Ranger Rocket."
He'd blocked it out, tried to forget. But this was who he was, under the sarcasm and snarls.

This open wound.
Even during the happy times, it festered inside. What was done to him.
What he'd do **back...**

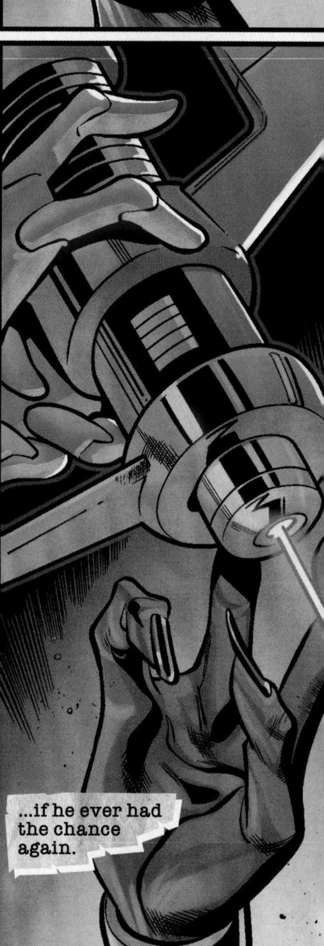
...if he ever had the chance again.

The surgical laser went up to 5,000 degrees if it had to.
Rocket figured it had to.
SUBJECT BEHAVIOR IS NOT--KRZZT--LOGICAL--
WE ARE--FZZT--MAKING SUBJECT BETTER--
YEAH? NICE JOB, TIN MAN.
I FEEL BETTER ALREADY.
Even so, something wasn't right.
tle details shifted and changed ound him. Like memories.
And where were the other animals?
Lylla and Wal? Blackjack and Uncle Pyko? His friends?
When had he lost them?

If he could find even one face from those days, maybe he could make sense of this. Just **one.**
OH FLARK.
Careful what you wish for.
Rocket knew the Hulk from the day--from the day **before** the day.
Gentle and green as a meadow. A guy with a temper, sure--but he'd never hurt a soul.
ROCKET.
But that guy wasn't this guy.
HERE TO ***WATCH?***
This was no meadow.
This was the **lake of fire.**
PUT...PUT HIM ***DOWN,*** HULK.
I'M ASKIN' ***NICE*** HERE
OKAY?

...FINE BY ME. I DON'T EVEN NEED TO TOUCH HIM.
ALL I NEED IS TIME.
THE HEARING LOSS IS THE LEAST OF IT. YOU'RE OLD, BARTON--OLDER EVERY DAY.
HOW MANY YEARS BEFORE YOUR AIM GOES?
HOW LONG BEFORE YOU'RE IN A REAL HOSPITAL? WITH THAT NEW HAWKEYE--YOU KNOW, THE ONE WHO'S BETTER THAN YOU ALREADY--
--SIGNING THE PAPERS TO SWITCH YOU OFF?
KNOW WHERE I'LL BE THEN? WHEN THEY BURY YOU? STILL ALIVE. STILL STRONG.
STILL IMMORTAL...
...
WAIT A SEC.
THIS... ISN'T A REAL HOSPITAL?
HNH.
COUNT YOUR FINGERS.

THEY'RE ALL BACK, RIGHT?
GET READY. HE'S MAKING HIS MOVE...
'CAUSE NONE OF THIS IS "REAL." NOT THE WAY YOU THINK, ANYWAY.
WHO?
In his gut, Rocket already knew.
He was no stranger to bad dreams.
THAT'S RIGHT, HULK!
ALL OF YOU ARE LOST--MAROONED IN MY REALM! TO SUFFER FOREVER--TORTURED ETERNALLY AT THE HANDS OF YOUR GREATEST FOE--
--NIGHTMARE!
It looked pretty bad-but Rocket figured there was still some angle, something he wasn't seeing yet...

omething
at made it
rse.
--NOW!
WHEREVER
YAGER SENT US--
E COAST IS CLEAR.
FORM ON ME,
EVERYONE.
LET'S TRY NOT
TO DRAW ATTENTION
TO OURSELVES UNTIL
WE--
UHHH--!
WANDA!
DAMN YOU,
VOYAGER!
OR
NOT.
WANDA,
ARE YOU
OKAY?
I'M BLIND,
SPECTRUM.
EVERYTHING WENT
DARK AFTER NYX
STRUCK MY
EYES...
TAKE MY
ARM AND I
WILL HELP
YOU.
WILL NOT HAVE
VENGEANCE
TAKEN FROM
ME!
HOOOM
WHAT'S
THAT
NOISE?
HERCULES IS
MOURNING.
HERC, WE
NEED YOU
FOCUSED.
MUST GET OUR BEARINGS
AND FIGURE OUT WHERE
VOYAGER HAS SENT
US-S-S-S-S-S--
--SSSSSSS.
VIZ?
J-J-JUST
A MINOR VARIANCE.
I'M REROUTING NEURAL
PATHWAYS TO
COMPENSATE...
YOUR
SYSTEMS ARE
DETERIORATING.
YES, BUT
WE WILL
PERSEVERE.
ENOUGH
CHATTER. THERE'S
LIGHT UP AHEAD.
LET'S GO.

OKAY. I'VE BEEN IN GALACTUS' HOUSE.
THIS IS MORE IMPRESSIVE.
IT SEEMS WE'RE IN OMNIPOTENCE CITY.

WHAT? WHAT IS THAT?
"THE MOST PEERLESS PIECE OF EARTH, I THINK, THAT E'ER THE SUN SHONE BRIGHT ON."
ITS BEAUTY MATTERS NOT. WE MUST PRESS ON.

SO, THE SUN STILL SHINES HERE?
THE LIGHT OF KNOWLEDGE SHALL NOT FADE 'TIL THE COSMOS CLOSES IN UPON ITSELF.
WAIT!
TH-THERE'S SOMETHING ELSE...
...SOMETHING GLOWING OUT THERE.
THERE'S ALL KINDS OF THINGS GLOWING, WANDA.
CAN YOU BE MORE SPECIFIC?
IT'S A SHAPE BURNING WITH DARK ENERGY, SOMEWHERE UP AHEAD.
IT'S THE ONLY THING I CAN SEE...
THAT CAN'T BE A COINCIDENCE.
LET ME SCOUT AHEAD AND SEE WHAT THAT IS--
DON'T. IT IS ALL TOO EASY TO LOSE YOURSELF HERE THIS PLACE IS MYTH-NOT SCIENCE.
THERE ARE NO COINCIDENCES OR RANDOM EVENTS, ONL FATE. THAT ENERGY MU BE WHAT VOYAGER SEN US TO FIND, SO FIND IT WE SHALL...
...AND THEN I WILL VISIT UNFETTERED WR UPON NYX AND FOUL CHILDRE
Something was off here

ALL YOU'VE GONE THROUGH WAS A MERE TASTE, PEONS! A SIMMERING SOUPÇON OF THE HORROR I CAN VISIT UPON YOU!
YOU WILL ASSIST ME IN MY GOALS--DO MY WILL--OR I WILL MAKE YOU SUFFER A NEVER-ENDING NIGHTMARE!
Rocket had pretty good hearing. And this guy didn't sound like an all-powerful dream king. Not quite.
He sounded like a salesman.
So what was he trying to sell?
I GOT A QUESTION. IF YOU'RE SO POWERFUL, HOW COME YOU NEED OUR HELP?
AND HOW COME I COULD BREAK OUTTA MY DREAM AND INTO HIS? WHAT WAS THAT ABOUT?
HNH.
HE'S GOT A POINT...
MAYBE BANNER'S ALREADY HAVING A NIGHTMARE.
I--I PLANNED THAT! OBVIOUSLY! GET BACK, YOU GREEN GARGOYLE!
WHY--WHY CAN'T I MAKE YOU AFRAID--
MAYBE I'M IT--
NO! WAIT!
WAIT!

JUST...HOLD ON, HULK. BEFORE THIS GETS OUT OF HAND...
BEHOLD ME AS I TRULY AM.
WEAKENED... AND EVIDENTLY EVEN MORE POWERLESS THAN I THOUGHT.
FIGURED AS MUCH.
START TALKING, NIGHTMARE. MAKE IT GOOD.
Nightmare made it good.
Long ago, he'd done a favor for Zeus.

Zeus had some kind of power crystal-- "The Night That May Yet Be." He wanted it hidden where nobody would ever look: With his enemy, hidden behind the "light of dreams," whatever that was.
In return, Zeus and his People would stay off Nightmare's turf.

And for thousands of years, that's how it was. Nightmare kept Zeus' MacGuffin in his fortress, out of harm's way--
--and the Greek Gods never bothered him again.

THOOM
?
Until one of them did.

Someone hadn't gotten Zeus' memo.
Hypnos, son of the Queen of Night. God of sleep.
LEGIONS OF THE SLEEPING-- *FORWARD!*
BRING DOWN THE WALLS!
THOOM
Including **dreamless** sleep.
Z
Z
Z
That meant any sleeping mind could be a soldier in his army--**immune** to Nightmare's power--
--and robbing him of the dreams that **sustained** him.
SO YOU *RAN?*
I'M STILL THERE. *AND* HERE. THE FORTRESS IS A *METAPHOR*, LIKE *EVERYTHING* IN DREAMS.
BUT EVEN SO, ITS WALLS WILL *CRUMBLE*...
...AND WHEN THEY *DO*, HYPNOS WILL *HAVE* HIS BAUBLE--AND EVERYTHING *ELSE* OF MINE. I AM TOO WEAK TO *STOP* HIM.
BUT NOT TOO WEAK TO *TORTURE* US.
YOU COULD HAVE ASKED FOR *HELP*--
NO. I DO NOT--I *WILL* NOT *BEG*.
DO YOU UNDERSTAND THE *HUMILIATION* OF THIS, CLINT BARTON? TO NEED *AID* FROM A *SWORN ENEMY?* FROM *ANY* MERE MORTALS?
THIS... THIS IS *MY* NIGHTMARE.

FINE. WE CAN'T LET HYPNOS GET HIS HANDS ON THAT... WHATEVER IT IS.
WE'LL HELP--
HEY! SPEAK FOR YOURSELF, CAPTAIN POINTY STICKS.

THIS TALL GLASS OF FLARK MILK JUST GOT DONE TORTURING US--NOW HE WANTS MY SERVICES?
TWO WORDS, UGLY: PAY ME.
HEY, THAT'S NOT HOW THE AVENGERS OPERATE--

I HAD A RUN-IN WITH THE REAL AVENGERS, BARTON. YOU WEREN'T THERE.
'CAUSE THEY DON'T WANT YOU.
SO SHUT UP. THE ADULTS ARE TALKING.

ROCKET'S RIGHT. YOU WANT MY HELP? IT'LL COST YOU.
RIDICULOUS. I TOLD YOU--MY POWER IS ALL BUT GONE. I AM A SHADOW OF MYSELF.
WHAT CAN I POSSIBLY OFFER YOU?

WHAT D
I EVEN H
LEFT?
HNH.
Something in that smile made Rocket uneasy.
He'd known Hulk when h was stupid.
But now, out of all of them, was the o one who k just wher he was...

...and where he wanted to be.
THIS WAY. I CAN SEE IT...
BE CAREFUL, WANDA.
YOU'VE BEEN HERE BEFORE?
YES. THIS IS THE CENTER OF INFINITY. THE NEXUS OF THE GODS.

OMNIPOTENCE CITY IS A REALM OF DIVINE FELLOWSHIP AND GOVERNANCE WHERE IMMORTALS FROM ALL CORNERS OF REALITY COME TO DEBATE, TO ALLY, TO MOURN.

IN ITS PARLIAMENT OF PANTHEONS, LAWS THAT AFFECT BILLIONS ARE ENACTED. WITHIN THE GENESIS BAZAAR, GODS BARTER THE DESTINIES OF ENTIRE GALAXIES.

FATE HAS GRANTED YOU AN IMMENSE HONOR, MY FRIENDS. NO MORTAL HAS EVER SET FOOT INSIDE OMNIPOTENCE CITY...

HOW. DARE. YOU.
...AND WERE IT UP TO THE LORD HIGH LIBRARIAN, NONE EVER WOULD.
START LOOKING.
GOOD SIR, WE'VE NO TIME TO WASTE. I BRING WITH ME--
I'M FAMILIAR WITH YOUR... LESSERS, HERCULES.
YOU'RE INSIDE THE HALLS OF THE ALL-KNOWING, FOR HEL'S SAKE. THERE ARE NO SURPRISES HERE.
THEN IF YOU ARE THE KEEPER OF ALL KNOWLEDGE, YOU'RE AWARE THAT THEIR INTRUSION IS NOT AN ACT OF MALICE.
APPARENTLY, MY FATHER ENTRUSTED YOU WITH THE SAFEKEEPING OF A FRAGMENT OF POWER.
WHERE IS IT NOW?
ALL-KNOWING AND ALL-TELLING ARE TWO DIFFERENT THINGS, HERCULES. I REALIZE NYX INTENDS TO COME FOR THE NIGHT THAT WAS, BUT I'VE HIDDEN IT WELL. THAT'S ALL YOU NEED TO KNOW.
AND YOU THINK CAN STOP HER TAKING IT? MASSACRES THERE ARE UPON HUNDRED IMMORTALS WHO HELP US! THEM!

GODS WAR AMONG THEMSELVES ALL THE TIME, HERCULES. THE PARLIAMENT DOES NOT INVOLVE ITSELF IN SUCH INTERNAL MATTERS.
THIS ISN'T MERELY AN OLYMPIAN PROBLEM, YOU FOOL! NYX THREATENS ALL REALITY!
BE THAT AS IT MAY, MY HANDS ARE TIED.
THE SHARD IS WELL HIDDEN, HE SAID. TELL ME...HOW DO YOU CONCEAL SOMETHING INSIDE A ROOM WHERE EVERYTHING IS KNOWN?
...
YOU DON'T LET GO OF IT.
THIS "FRAGMENT"... THIS, I CAN SEE!
HERCULES, IT'S AROUND HIS NECK!

IS IT, NOW.
THANK YOU EVER SO MUCH.
WE'LL TAKE IT FROM HERE.
OH NO...
...NO, NO, NO...
NYX DIDN'T BLIND YOU, WANDA!
SHE TURNED YOU INTO HER EYES--!
APATE AND DOLOS! GODS OF DECEIT AND TRICKERY--THEY'LL TRY TO SEPARATE US! PROTECT THE LIBRARIAN!
COPY THAT.

I'LL IN--
-OFFENSE--
WHERE DID THEY GO?!
MORTAL, TAKE GREAT CARE! THE FOG OF DOLOS CORRUPTS THE SENSES OF ANYONE IT TOUCHES!
YOU'LL NOT EASILY PENETRATE ITS COVER!
WHAT OF APATE?
WHAT'S HER SPECIALTY?
LIES.
HER DAGGERS CUT THROUGH FLESH--

--THROUGH REASON--
--THROUGH SANITY!
THHP
THHP
NO, LIBRARIAN
FINALLY... I CAN THINK CLEARLY.
THE AVENGERS FAILED TO SAVE OLYMPUS. THEY BEAR THE RESPONSIBILITY.
SO THE LAST SON OF OLYMPUS MUST BALANCE THE SCALES...
...BY KILLING THE ALL...

SPOTLIGHT ON: JOSHUA JAMES SHAW

elcome back, True Believers! Last week, we showed off the dazzling designs that Joshua James aw settled on for Nyx and her little bundles of joy. But it's always fun to look at what could have en, so take a gleeful gander at these alternate designs, accompanied by delightful design notes from Joshua himself!

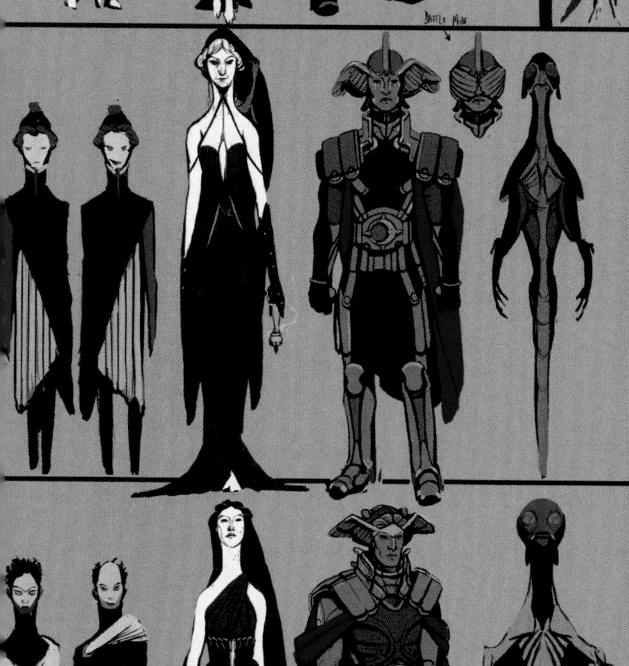

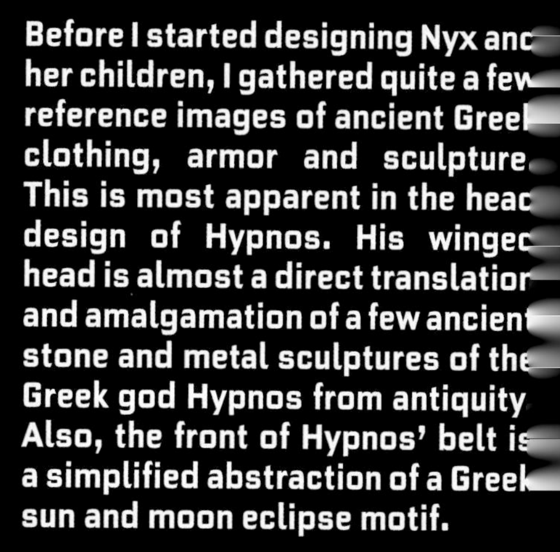

Before I started designing Nyx and her children, I gathered quite a few reference images of ancient Greek clothing, armor and sculpture. This is most apparent in the head design of Hypnos. His winged head is almost a direct translation and amalgamation of a few ancient stone and metal sculptures of the Greek god Hypnos from antiquity. Also, the front of Hypnos' belt is a simplified abstraction of a Greek sun and moon eclipse motif.

I was very conscious that any new design that is meant to be derived from ancient times yet is meant to exist in the present day might come off looking a little silly (Google "ancient Greek hoplite"). Because of this I wanted to fuse a little modern fashion into their design while not letting that overcome what makes it "Greek." Along with this (and most importantly when designing ANYTHING "Marvel") I try to stay true to what I see as the major component that makes Golden and Silver Age designs sing through to present day. I think it's as simple as a BOLD and ICONIC blocking of color and value. The details can be changed over and over throughout the years and the character will always shine through as long as the iconic nature of the design is retained. And I think that ICONIC design lives within those limited value and color palettes and the graphic designs we create with them.

Joshua James Shaw

4

IN THE BEGINNING, THERE WAS DARKNESS.
A SILENT DREAM.
IN SUCH STILLNESS I WAS BORN.
BEFORE THE LIGHT.
THE EMPTINESS WAS PURE.
ITS POTENTIAL WAS ENDLESS.
IT WOULD NOT LAST.
THE LIGHT BEGAN TO GROW.
HARSH.
UNYIELDING.
ZEUS.
GOD OF SKY AND IGHTNING. SON OF E GALACTIC TITANS.
LOUD AND BRIGHT.
HE COULD NOT STAND TO BE ALONE WITH ME.

THUS CAME OLYMPUS.
AND WITH IT, MANY OLYMPIANS.

THE GODS WERE ABUNDANT, AND THEY CARVED UP THE DARKNESS TO MAKE THEIR KINGDOM GLITTER AND THEIR STORIES SHINE.
STORIES OF HEROISM.
STORIES OF HEARTBREAK.
A PETTY PAGEANTRY TO WHILE AWAY THE CENTURIES.

THE GODS HAD CHILDREN AND IT MADE THEM HAPPY.
I WONDERED IF I COULD EVER FEEL SUCH JOY.
I DREAMT OF DARKNESS ONCE MORE. THE STILLNESS OF SLUMBER.
MY FIRSTB ARRIVED TH NIGHTS HEN
HYPNOS.
THE GO OF SLEE
MY BOY TRIED TO FIND HIS PLACE IN THE LIGHT BUT, LIKE ME, HE FOUND ITS COUNTENANCE A POOR FIT FOR HIS DESIRES.
LOYAL AND STOIC, HE WOULD GATHER AN ARMY OF SLEEPERS TO GUARD THE NIGHT FROM ENEMIES...

AND TO VATCH VER MY REAMS.
ARMY OF SLEEP! NIGHTMARE'S FORTRESS IS ALMOST OURS! IN MOTHER'S NAME!
DREAMLESS--FALL BACK! IMAGINATORS FORWARD! SIEGE MACHINES--READY!
NIGHTMARE'S REALM.
BUT AS THE MORTALS KNEW SLEEP, SO THEY KNEW DREAMS OF THEIR OWN...
THIS IS A MOVIE...? BUT...I'M IN THE MOVIE...
I'M SO LATE FOR CLASS.
FOR NYX! AND FOR HER VENGEANCE!
FIRE!
...VISIONS LIT BY THE SPARK OF IMAGINATION...
...PROPELLED INTO REALITY.
EARTH, AGE OF BEGAN.
HUMANKIND'S OWN LIGHT...LIT AT THEIR COMMAND.

NIGHT AND DARK WERE BANISHED TO THE OUTER SIDE, WITH ALL THE UNKNOWNS HUMANITY FEARED...
'FRAID AM I, OLD-MAN. NIGHT, IS. TIGER GOD HUNTS...
NO NIGHT OR TIGER IN HERE.
HEARKEN TO TELLER NOW. TELLER HAS TELLINGS...
AND AS BEFORE, WITH THE LIGHT CAME THE STORIES.
MORTAL MAGICIANS, USING THEIR MAGIC WORDS TO DISPEL THE NIGHT'S TERRORS...
TELL OF THE NIGHT-WITCH, SKALD! AND OF THE GOD-KING WHO ENDED HER DARKNESS!
WOULD YOU KNOW MORE, MY CHIEF?
ONCE UPON A TIME...

...AND CAGE THE NIGHT'S MYSTERIES.
HAIL, CHILDREN OF ZEUS!
GRANT LOVELY SONG AND CELEBRATE THE HOLY RACE OF THE DEATHLESS GODS...
LINES WERE DRAWN. GOOD AND EVIL DEFINED.
THEIR WORDS AND SYMBOLS SHAPED ZEUS AND HIS CHILDREN--EVER MORE, EVER GROWING--INTO HEROES.

WHAT DID THAT MAKE ME AND MINE?

WITH EACH NEW LEGION OF FOLLOWERS THE OLYMPIANS PULLED INTO THEIR BRIGHT HALLS, I FELT MY RAGE GROW.
THEY NEVER WANTED ME AMONG THEM. THEY FEARED THE POWER OF DARKNESS.
ANOTHER DREAM. MY MIND FILLED WITH BETRAYAL.
E TWINS ME THUSLY.
APATE AND DOLOS.
DECEIT AND TRICKERY.
ECHOES OF MY FRUSTRATION, THEY WOULD NEVER BELIEVE THE LIES OF OLYMPUS.
CONFLICT BECAME INEVITABLE...
...AND MY CHILDREN WERE BRED FOR IT...

...AS WEAPONS OF WAR.
OMNIPOTENCE CITY.
HERCULES, WAIT! THE TWINS ARE CORRUPTING YOUR MIND! WE MUST NOT--
THWAM
VISION!
SPECTRUM, WHAT'S HAPPENING?
NOTHING GOOD, WANDA! SOUNDS LIKE VISION'S SYSTEMS ARE GLITCHING AGAIN, AND I CAN'T CUT THROUGH THIS FOG! WHERE'S THE LIBRARIAN?
NOT A WORD.
MORTALS! IF NOT FOR YOUR WHINING AND MEWLING, ALWAYS BEGGING FOR MY HELP, I WOULD HAVE BEEN ON OLYMPUS!
I WOULD HAVE SAVED MY FAMILY!
HER-C%-CU--
--FAM-- WE ARE--Y%UR FAMI-MI-MI--

FIND THE LIBRARIAN!
I'LL TRY TO SNAP HERCULES OUT OF THAT SPELL!
OH?
YOU'RE CERTAINLY WELCOME TO TRY.
AFTER ALL--
--HE'LL BE AFTER YOU NEXT.
NOT MUCH OF A CHALLENGE, THIS GROUP.
HUMANS. WHAT DID YOU EXPECT?
HOLD HIM WHILE I CARVE.

LET HIM BE.
SURPRISE. SINCE WE'RE ALL LINKED TO YOUR MOTHER'S POWER, YOU AREN'T HIDDEN TO ME.
SPECTRUM, I HAVE THE TWINS! CAN YOU SHOCK HERCULES OUT OF IT?
NOW THAT THERE'S ONLY ONE OF HIM, SURE.
JUST A CASE OF FINDING THE RIGHT STROBE FREQUENCY...
UNGH!
MY MIND... WHAT HAVE I DONE? FORGIVE ME, MY FRIE--
?

THERE YOU ARE.

AND THEN, AT LAST, WE FOUGHT.
DARKNESS AGAINST THE LIGHT.
MY TRUTH AGAINST THEIR LIES.

THE OLYMPIANS, SQUABBLERS AND MEDDLERS FOR ETERNITY, SOMEHOW FOUND COMMON GROUND IN THEIR HATRED OF ME.
THE NIGHT WAS CRUSHED UNDER THEIR GOLDEN HEELS.
DEFEAT WAS JUST THE BEGINNING OF OUR TORMENT.
THE WORDS OF ZEUS DROVE INTO MY BRAIN LIKE A SEARING BRAND.
"THE NIGHT IS YOURS NO LONGER.
"I SHALL BREAK IT THRICE AND CAST THE SHARDS BEYOND YOUR REACH.
"NEVER AGAIN SHALL YOU POSSESS THEM."
THE NIGHT THAT WAS.
THE NIGHT THAT IS.
THE NIGHT THAT YET MAY BE.
MY SOUL LAID BARE AND TAKEN FROM ME.
MY NAME FORBIDDEN AND FORGOTTEN.

AND THEN, THE TOMB.
"THE DARKNESS YOU CRAVED IS NOW YOUR PRISON.
"AS LONG AS THE SUN SHINES UPON THE EARTH, FOR YOU THERE SHALL BE NO ROAD HOME."

THE SILENCE AND STILLNESS WAS NOW A PIT OF HOWLING DESPAIR.
NO MORE DREAMS, ONLY NIGHTMARES.
AND FROM THOSE GHTMARES, MY FOURTH ND MOST POWERFUL CHILD WAS BIRTHED...
OIZYS.
THE MISERY.
MY HATRED MADE MANIFEST.
THESE REFLECTIONS OF MY EBONY EXISTENCE BOUND WITH ME, TRAPPED FOR ALL TIME.
LOST IN OUR SORROW, WE HAD ONLY EACH OTHER.
MOST WOULD HAVE PRAYED FOR MADNESS TO RELEASE THEM.
I PRAYED FOR REVENGE.

WHERE GO GODS AND COSMIC BEINGS, NOTHING IS IMPOSSIBLE.
FOR A BRIEF TIME, THE EARTH WAS STOLEN FROM ITS FAVORED SPOT BENEATH THE SUN'S ILLUMINATION.
AND THUS, THE SPELL OF IMPRISONMENT WAS BROKEN.
I WAS FREE.
FREE TO REGAIN ALL THAT WAS TAKEN...AND SO MUCH MORE.

THE OLYMPIANS,
HE MORTALS, THE
NIVERSE ITSELF...
AFTER AN ETERNITY OF MISTREATMENT, THEY HAVE ALL BEEN SPOILED.
OUR ONLY HOPE NOW IS A RETURN TO THE SILENCE.
AN END TO THE LIGHT.
I SHALL MAKE IT LIMITLESS.
EMPTY.
PURE.
IN THE NEW BEGINNING, THERE SHALL BE DARKNESS AGAIN...

NO THREAT.
NO THREAT AT ALL.
WHEN THE STORY OF THIS MOMENT IS WRITTEN IN YOUR BOOKS, LIBRARIAN, MAKE SURE IT SAYS THIS:
YEAAAAGGH
THE QUEEN OF NIGHT FOUND THE NIGHT THAT WAS...
...AND SHE BARELY BROKE A SWEAT.

...
I HEAR YOU, MOTHER.
YOU HAVE THE NIGHT THAT WAS...

KROOOOM

...AND SOON I WILL HAVE THE NIGHT THAT MAY YET BE.
DO YOU HEAR ME, NIGHTMARE? COME OUT! FACE YOUR BETTER!
YOUR CASTLE IS FALLEN! AND YOUR NIGHT WILL BE MINE--
NOT YET.

WHAT?
SEE...THAT'S MY CASTLE NOW.
AND THE NIGHT...

...THE NIGHT IS MY TIME.

...E ASSEMBLY

...elcome back, True Believers, to THE ASSEMBLY! In honor of Nyx's villainous origin this week ... asked our witty wordsmiths to wax poetic about their favorite Marvel villains. Who did they choose? Read on and find out!

...th so many amazing villains to choose from in the Marvel pantheon, it's hard to pick a ...vorite. Is it the Green Goblin, star of the most suspenseful Silver Age Marvel story o... ... (SPECTACULAR SPIDER-MAN MAGAZINE #2)? Is it Dormammu, who sports one of the ...est character designs of all time (from DOCTOR STRANGE)? Is it the Kangaroo (nope)? ...hile I hate to go for the obvious, who else could it be but Doctor Doom? I'm a sucker for ...ories about enemies who could have been friends. I get a kick out of villains who are ...marter than I am. That he's often legally untouchable as the ruler of his own kingdom ...as a masterstroke idea from Stan Lee and Jack Kirby. And most of all, I love a borderline ...elusional villain (Seriously, his vaunted "nobility" is baloney--it comes and goes purely ... it suits him. Plus, I'd swear to you if you waterboarded me that the "horrible facia... ...car" that drove him mad was about an inch long.) Make Mine Doom.

Mark Waid

...his is tricky, because I have a deep love for villains who make face turns and show ...e good in them--Magneto, Loki, Molecule Man, Sandman, Kaluu, Absorbing Man and ...tania, Galactus--even the above-mentioned Doc Doom! Heck, in this very comic, we ...ave Hawkeye, Scarlet Witch and Voyager! (Not to mention the Hulk!) It's part of Marvel's ...NA that the villains are just as complicated as the heroes--but what about villains who ...eep it villainous? Who don't deviate from the path of the costumed crook? Let me presen... ...erhaps the greatest example of these...THE DEATH THROWS, a collective of villains ...emed entirely around juggling. I cannot stress enough that, unless you too have based ...our entire villain persona around juggling, YOU CANNOT JOIN THE DEATH THROWS. It'd ...reak the whole pun.

...nd yes, it's easy to laugh. It's easy to mock. But these visionary men and women--led by ...eir leader, Ringleader, who juggles rings--have turned a simple crime gang into a shared ...tistic space. When they walk into a bank or diamond exchange, it's not just a robbery... ...s a performance--and in the end, it's not even for the crowds. They do what they do fo... ...ach other, because the only people who truly understand juggling-themed super villains ...e other juggling-themed super villains. And maybe that's our loss.

Al Ewing

...oki is way up there for me. The God of Mischief runs the gamut from an absolutely ...eartless deity willing to destroy anything or anyone in service of his machinations to a ...isunderstood, empathetic child trying to change his dark and tragic fate. The fact that ...hose opposing interpretations, and everything in between, work well and still feel like ...oki shows how dynamic and interesting a character he can be... And the fact that he's ...ght here beside me as I type this, whispering in my ear with a knife at my throat, doesn't ...urt either.

Jim Zub

5

OMNIPOTENCE CITY.
THE DARKNESS DRAWS EVER CLOSER NOW...
...AND WE'RE HELPLESS TO STOP IT.

HERCULES' LEGENDARY RAGE THREATENS TO BOIL OVER, BUT IT HAS NOWHERE TO GO.
DAMN YOU, NYX!
I WILL AVENGE THE OLYMPIANS AND SEE YOU SLAIN!
NYX, THE QUEEN OF NIGHT, IS IN CONTROL.
SHE AND HER CHILDREN DISPATCHED US WITH EASE, AND WITH THAT PIECE OF POWER SHE HOLDS SHE'LL BECOME EVEN STRONGER.
THESE SHARDS ZEUS CREATED TO DIMINISH MY GLORY... HOW DO I ACCESS THEIR POWER ONCE MORE?
DO I SHATTER IT? INGEST IT?
IT'S A STRANGE SORT OF PUZZLE, ISN'T IT?

SPECTRUM'S ENERGY FORM CAN'T ESCAPE THIS MAGICAL PRISON.
VOYAGER IS BEING CONTROLLED.
YOUR MIND IS WEAK
YOU'RE NUMB
VISION IS DYING...HIS SYSTEM RIDDLED WITH MALFUNCTIONS AND HIS BODY BATTERED.

ND ME?
NYX TOOK MY SIGHT AND USED ME TO HELP FIND HER SHARD.
ALL I CAN "SEE" IS HER POWER...
...AND THAT GROWING DARKNESS.
I KNOW A SPELL THAT MIGHT BREAK THESE BONDS, BUT WITHOUT MY EYES, I CAN'T TRACE THE SIGILS NEEDED TO ACTIVATE IT.
NO ONE ELSE CAN SEE WHAT I SEE...
WAIT...
MONICA?
WANDA, PLEASE TELL ME YOU HAVE A BRILLIANT PLAN.
HAVE YOU EVER WANTED TO BE A WITCH?
"SO, ROCKET...I'M NOT SAYING I EVER WANTED THIS..."

NIGHTMARE'S REALM.
...BUT IS IT BAD THAT I'M KIND OF ENJOYING MYSELF?
I DON'T KNOW, BARTON.
MAYBE?
SLEEPERS! KEEP--KEEP THE GREEN DEMON BUSY!
Y-YOUR COMMANDER WILL--WILL BRAVELY FETCH THE SHARD OF NIGHT FROM NIGHTMARE'S CASTLE--
HNH.
YEAH, YOU BETTER RUN, HYPNOS.

IT'S LIKE-- WE'RE IN A DREAM. ONE OF THIS IS REAL, O I CAN CUT LOOSE AND NOT HURT ANYBODY.
FEELS KINDA LIKE SPACE INVADERS...

SPACE INVADERS?
WHAT'S THAT? SOME EARTH THING?

IT'S AN OLD VIDEO GAME. YOU HAVE TO KILL ALL THE PACE ALIENS BEFORE, UH...THEY SET FOOT ON EARTH SOIL...
PRESENT COMPANY EXCLUDED, I MEAN...

OH, THANK YOU. I FEEL SO, SO WELCOME IN YOUR NEIGHBORHOOD.
YOU KNOW THIS IS WHY THE WHOLE GALAXY THINKS YOU SUCK, RIGHT?

LOOK, I IDN'T COME UP WITH THE--
OH NO.

BARTON?
HOLY FLARK--

Z
WHOKK
--IT'S THE REAL HAWKEYE!

Z
KATE--IT'S ME, KATE! IT'S CLINT! WAKE UP!
ARE--ARE YOU SLEEPING IN YOUR CLOTHES? IT'S PAST NOON, KATE!

WHAT TIME DID YOU GET IN LAST NIGHT-- OWW!

Z
SHE'S LITERALLY BEATING ME IN HER SLEEP.
OKAY, ACE-IN-THE-HOLE TIME-- GOLIATH SERUM, TAKE ME AWAY--

HUH?
I HAD IT RIGHT HERE-- WHERE DID IT--

KZLOW
GAAHH!
YOU-- YOU SHOT HER--
WHAT? YOU SAI THIS WAS REAL--
WHAT IF I'M WRONG? WHAT IF IT IS?

THEN I GUESS WE'RE ALL SONS OF KRUTAKS, BARTON.
WHERE'D THE BIG GUY GO?

THE TASK IS DONE!
THE NIGHT THAT MAY YET BE IS IN MY HAND!
THE BATTLE IS ENDED-- AND I HAVE WON!
I'VE WON, DO YOU HEAR?
THAT MEANS YOU HAVE TO STOP!
MOTHER!
MOTHER, WHERE ARE YOU?
"SHE'S CONCENTRATING ON HER SHARD, SO WE'VE GOT A MOMENT."

I HEARD ABOUT THE TRICK YOU USED WHEN YOU FOUGHT SHUMA-GORATH.* I CAN GUIDE YOU THIS TIME.
THE GLYPHS? I CAN SHAPE MY LIGHT FORM, YES, BUT I CAN'T WORK OFF JUST A DESCRIPTION, CAN I?
*IN MIGHTY AVENGERS #3. --TOM
NOR CAN I DRAW SUCH EXACTING SHAPES BLIND. BUT IF YOU TRANSFORM INTO NEURAL ELECTRICITY--
--MAYBE I CAN ENTER YOUR MIND AND SEE YOUR THOUGHTS?
BRACE YOURSELF. THIS MAY HURT.
"HURT" IS AN UNDERSTATEMENT. IT'S A SEIZURE.
NYAAGGH!
AND THEN I HEAR HER VOICE IN MY HEAD.
WANDA?
I NEED YOU TO COPY THE SIGILS I'M PICTURING. COPY THEM PRECISELY.
THIS IS A COMPLEX SPELL REQUIRING CERTAIN VISUAL COMPONENTS--AND I'LL ONLY HAVE A MOMENT TO CAST IT.
HERCULES, VISION--BE READY.

I'M INTRIGUED BY SPECTRUM'S NEW LEVELS OF POWER.
BY BLOOD AND BONE OF OSTRUM...
AND I KNOW VISION WELL ENOUGH TO GUESS WHAT HE'S THINKING, BECAUSE HE'S WRESTLED WITH SOMETHING SIMILAR THE WHOLE TIME I'VE KNOWN HIM:
...'GAINST ENEMY OF NIGHT...
"IF A BEING LIKE SPECTRUM CAN CHANGE FORM AS EASILY AS A THOUGHT...IF ONE CAN LEAVE FLESH AND BLOOD BEHIND...
...TURN BLACK TO GRAY, TURN GRAY TO GOLD...
"...THEN HOW MUCH OF THEIR ORIGINAL HUMANITY IS LEFT?"
A QUESTION FOR LATER.
...TURN DARKNESS INTO LIGHT!

FORGET MOTHER NIGHT! CONCENTRATE ON HER KIDS!
TRUST ME!
VERY WELL.
=KOFF=
THA-WHOOM
APATE, WAS IT? NASTY WORK, THOSE KNIVES.
I IMAGINE YOU AND DOLOS THERE ARE AWFULLY FORMIDABLE...
...AS LONG AS YOU CAN LAY A HAND ON YOUR OPPONENTS!

KILL.
THEM.
FRIEND VOYAGER, ARE YOU INJURED?
JUST OFF-- JUST AKEN. I--
LOOK OUT!
SURRENDER
RRENDER
RRENDER
YOU CANNOT WIN
NOT WIN
CANNOT WIN
!
SUCCUMB
SUCCUMB
SUCCUMB
OIZYS. YOU--
--YOU TRAFFIC IN--
--IN DESPAIR-- DO YOU--?

THEN YOU ARE A FOOL TO FACE A MAN WITH NOTHING LEFT TO LOSE!
AGAIN, BECAUSE MY BLINDNESS IS LINKED TO NYX, SHE AND HER OFFSPRING ARE NOT ALTOGETHER HIDDEN FROM ME.
I IMAGINE THE FRUSTRATION APATE FEELS FIGHTING AN IMMATERIAL WOMAN.
I CAN FEEL THE SOLAR ENERGY THAT VISION, TAPPING DANGEROUSLY DEEP INTO HIS RESERVE OF POWER, UNLEASHES AGAINST DOLOS.
THIS IS WORKING. THERE'S A REASON I TOLD THE OTHERS TO ATTACK NOT NYX BUT HER CHILDREN.
THEY'RE PROVIDING ANY MAGICIAN'S GREATEST ADVANTAGE:
MISDIRECTION

NO!
I HAVE NO PLAN. ONLY CERTAINTY THAT NYX CANNOT HAVE THAT WHICH SHE SEEKS--
--AND HOPE-- THAT VOYAGER IS WATCHING--
WHAT DO YOU THINK YOU'RE DOING?!
WANDA! THE SHARD!
--AND THAT SHE'LL SEE WHAT HAS TO BE DONE.

WANDA, KEEP IT SAFE!
A MOMENT OF WEIGHTLESSNESS... AND THEN I FEEL MYSELF FALLING--
YOU ODIOUS LITTLE INSECT--!
MOTHER, NO
MOTHER, NO
MOTHER, NO
SHE MUST TELL US
TELL US
TELL US
WHERE SHE SENT THE FRAGMENT
THE FRAGMENT
THE FRAGMENT
HYPNOS, YOUR SIBLINGS HAVE FAILED ME!
COME TO ME! I MUST HAVE YOUR SHARD NOW!
DO YOU UNDERSTAND ME? COME TO ME AT ONCE SO THAT WE MAY--
HYPNOS!

MOTHER-- I--
--I'M SORRY--
I--I TRIED--
YEAH.
YOU HAD A BIG DAY, LITTLE MAN.
NOW GO TO SLEEP.
KRAAKK

HYPNOSSSSS!
ENOUGH OF THIS!
MORTALS--
--YOU'VE NO *CONCEPT* OF HOW *MERCIFUL* I HAVE BEEN THUS FAR! WELL--

--LET THIS BE YOUR LESSON!
OH...
...OH NO...

"NO!"
WHERE AM-- WHO--?! STAY BACK!
KRAK
AHHH!
BEAUTIFUL, BUT FOOLISH!
SHE'S GOT SOME KINDA CRYSTAL...
I BET THIS'L BE WORTH FA SILVER IN TH MARKET!
NO, PLEASE! DON'T! YOU... YOU DON'T UNDERSTAND!
I'M... I'M LOST AND--
LOST AND DEAD, NOW.
HEH-- BETTER LUCK IN THE NEXT LIFE!
ROBBING A HELPLESS WENCH?
YOU ZAMORAN SCUM ARE ALL THE SAME...

YIPPING DOGS OKING FOR AN EASY MEAL!
ET BA-- AAHH!
THE AIR IS HOT... HUMID...

FEAST ON THIS, MONGREL!
AHHHH!
SHUNK
CRUNCH
SAND BETWEEN MY FINGERS...
...CHOKING SOUNDS OF VIOLENCE.

OH!
THE STENCH OF METAL AND SWEAT.
FWUMP

FWHAM
NGG--!
MY HEAD IS RINGING...

RUN!
HE CAN'T CATCH US ALL!
...BUT I MUST FIND THE SHARD BEFORE IT'S...

REST NOW, WOMAN.
I WILL CARRY YOU...

...THIS CIMMERIAN HAS ENOUGH STRENGTH FOR US BOTH.

onan the Barbarian."

pe out those words and they instantly pull me into a vortex of happy memories high adventure.

much as J.R.R. Tolkien set the pace for our mainstream perception of fantasy n his sweeping stories about hobbits, elves and dragons, Robert E. Howard ped into something more visceral. Conan carved his way into my subconscious n somewhere dark. He showed me the murky depths of low fantasy: a peerless file of pain and peril etched in pulp.

Cimmerian's stories are about morally dubious miscreants struggling to vive in a mad world they will never fully understand. His words and deeds tured my imagination as a kid and they still engage me now because they're nal--an alchemical stew of relentless violence and a bewildered curiosity fo unknown and the unwanted.

an and Dungeons & Dragons burned a brand in my brain and created a template what sword & sorcery was all about: good people making bad choices, warriors ting against insane odds, and misplaced courage. The kind of misplaced rage that makes you look death in the face and laugh.

first professional comic credit arrived in 2003, recoloring Barry Windsor-th pages for Dark Horse's *Chronicles of Conan* collections, which themselves e reprints of the original Marvel Conan stories. Twelve years later, I co-wrote *an Red Sonja* with Gail Simone and thought that would be my only chance to be rd for the barbarian.

nkfully not. When Tom Brevoort told me we'd be able to use Conan in our oming Avengers weekly story, I contemplated how I would convince Mark Waid Al Ewing that those Hyborean scenes with Wanda were already mine. Even email, I think they knew. The maps, lore and other reference material I flooded n with probably helped too.

uldn't help it. Conan's my guy. I wouldn't be here if it weren't for the Barbarian Thief, the Wanderer, the Adventurer, the Buccaneer, the Warrior, the Usurper Conqueror, the Freebooter, the Avenger...

an is the original antihero, the sellsword survivor who became a king by his hand. He's the savage template for every Wolverine, Punisher, Elektra or ter Soldier-style character in literature, film or games. His mirth and myth are end, bigger than any comic that tries to contain him. Does that sound cynical? not. It's just the truth, by Crom, brought to you on the keen edge of a blade ded by a man with nothing left to lose...

Jim Zub

FOR CONAN PROPERTIES INTERNATIONAL
President: Fred Malmberg • Executive Vice President: Jay Zetterberg
Chief Operation Officer: Steve Booth

6

NO!
NO!
NOOOOO!
THE WITCH'S NIGHTMARES GROW WORSE.

THE BARBARIAN'S HAND GRIPS HIS SWORD HILT TIGHT AS THE WITCH SCREAMS, AWAKENED BY VISIONS THAT CUT HER TO THE QUICK.
ARE YOU--?
NO! I'M...
I'M ALL RIGHT, CONAN.

THE CIMMERIAN HAS HEARD SUCH CRIES BEFORE...
...A BURNING PAIN THAT ERUPTS FROM WITHIN ONE'S SOUL.
HE KNOWS IT WELL.

THERE ARE NO WORDS OF SOLACE THE CIMMERIAN CAN GIVE, SO HE FOCUSES INSTEAD ON THE IMMEDIATE.
YOUR WOUND IS STILL TENDER.
IT'S PROBABLY A CONCUSSION...
A WHAT?

WE'VE TRAVELED FOR THREE DAYS, YET I SENSE THAT BACK IN MY WORLD MERE MOMENTS HAVE PASSED.
WHEREVER YOU COME FROM, RED WITCH, IT LIES OUT OF REACH.

HEN CONAN FOUND
E BLIND SORCERESS,
E WAS BEING
MBUSHED BY BANDITS.
HE SLEW A PAIR OF HER ATTACKERS, WHILE THE REST SCATTERED LIKE RATS.
SHE TOLD THE BARBARIAN THE TREASURE STOLEN FROM HER IS WORTH MORE THAN ANYTHING A DOZEN MERCHANT LORDS OF BAALUR COULD AFFORD, SO HE AGREED TO HELP HER GET IT BACK...
...IN RETURN FOR A HALF SHARE OF THE FORTUNE, OF COURSE.
ONCE THE SHARD IS WITHIN OUR GRASP, IT'S CRUCIAL THAT I DO NOT LOOK AT IT... NOT EVEN FOR AN INSTANT.
I THOUGHT YOU WERE BLIND.
IN A MANNER OF SPEAKING. MY SIGHT HAS BEEN TAKEN BY A GREAT EVIL AND IT'S IMPORTANT THAT SHE NOT SEE THE SHARD THROUGH MY EYES.
FAIR ENOUGH.
FINDING THE BANDITS MEANS CROSSING THE ARANZA DESERT, A DESOLATE PLANE OF SCORCHING SAND.
WHAT FEW TRAVELERS THEY COME ACROSS IN THEIR TREK HEW TO TWO DISTINCT IDEOLOGIES--
SURVIVORS...
...AND SAVAGES.
AND THERE ARE OTHER THREATS BENEATH THE DUNES AS WELL...

MONSTERS!
DEADLY CREATURES FROM TIMES LONG FORGOTTEN AND LANDS LONG BURIED.

THAT'S RIGHT, CLAWED ONE... I AM YOUR PREY!

THIS CIMMERIAN-BORN WILL KEEP YOUR GAZE AND CARVE YOUR INNARDS!

THE SIGHTLESS SORCERESS COULD HEAR THE HORSE'S PAINFUL CRIES AND USED THEM TO FIND HER TARGET.

MY COMPANION MAY BE BLIND, BUT YOU MUST BE DEAF...

...I SAID, LOOK AT ME!

CONAN?
READY YOUR FOUL MAGICS, WITCH...AND AIM THEM TOWARD THE SOUND OF MY VOICE!
I'LL TRY, BUT--
YOU WILL, WOMAN, ELSE WE'LL BOTH END UP SUN-BLEACHED SKELETONS IN THE MIDDLE OF NOWHERE!
DO IT...
NOW!
HA!
A DEMONIC BOLT FOR A DEMONIC BEAST!
WELL MET, WANDA EARTHBORN.

WITHOUT OUR MOUNT, WE WON'T GET FAR...
THE NOMADS WHO PASSED US EARLIER FOLLOW A PREDICTABLE ROUTE. THEY'VE STOPPED FOR THE NIGHT. IF WE'RE CAREFUL, WE CAN CATCH THEM AND BARTER FOR ONE OF THEIR STEEDS.
BARTER? WHAT DO WE HAVE TO TRADE?
MY STEEL OR YOUR BEAUTY. EITHER WAY, THEY'LL HELP US OR I'LL CUT THEM ALL DOWN.
YOU CAN BE QUITE CRUEL, CONAN.
I AM WHATEVER CROM NEEDS ME TO BE TO SURVIVE.
WHO IS THIS CROM?
GOD OF THE GREAT MOUNTAIN.
HE GIVES MY PEOPLE THE POWER TO STRIVE AND TO SLAY.
AND YOU PRAY TO HIM?
CROM DOESN'T NEED PRAYERS AND I WOULD NEVER ASK.
SO, THIS IS YOUR LIFE... MONEY AND MURDER?
IT IS NOW.
BUT IT WAS NOT ALWAYS THIS WAY?
EAT THE HORSE MEAT WHILE IT'S WARM.
THEN WE'LL BE OFF.

THE WITCH'S ENCHANTMENTS DAZZLED THE DESERT TRAVELERS AND A DEAL WAS QUICKLY STRUCK.
NO NEED FOR THREATS OR THUGGERY.
WO MORE DAYS CROSS VIND-BLASTED AND STRETCHING FF TOWARD HE HORIZON...
CONAN KNEW THE BANDITS WHO STOLE THE CRYSTAL COULD NOT HAVE MADE IT FAR.
SOON ENOUGH, WITH PRESSURE EXERTED IN A MANNER THE CIMMERIAN FOUND PLEASING, A WAY FORWARD REVEALED ITSELF.
THE THIEVES HAD SET UP CAMP ON THE EDGE OF THE ILLITESE RIVER.
YOU GO FIRST AND FIND THE SHARD.
ONCE YOU'VE HIDDEN IT FROM MY SIGHT, I'LL MOVE IN TO ASSIST YOU.
AND THUS THE SWORDSMAN AND SORCERESS PREPARED TO STEAL BACK THAT WHICH HAD ALREADY BEEN STOLEN...

THE STENCH OF FRESH BLOOD.
THE SOUND OF WIND RIPPLING ACROSS TORN TARPS AND LOOSE FABRIC.
THE THIEVES HAD ALREADY BEEN LOOTED.
IT SEEMS WE'RE NOT THE ONLY ONES SEARCHING FOR YOUR PRECIOUS TREASURE...
ARE THEY--
DEAD?
INDEED.

OUR BANDITS FOUGHT MEN IN RED ROBES... AND A FLOCK OF CROWS AS WELL...
...A STRANGE COMBINATION.

WHAT'S THIS THEN?
YOU FOUND SOMETHING?

I'VE SEEN HIS MARKING BEFORE...
UHHHH--
THOUGH MANY YEARS HAD PASSED, SOME SYMBOLS REFUSED TO FADE.
THIS STYLIZED SKULL STILL BURNED LIKE A BUTCHER'S BRAND IN THE BARBARIAN'S MIND.

YOU SERVE THE NIGHT-GOD.
EYES OF MIDNIGHT COME FOR US ALL...

YOU KNOW HIM?
I KNOW HIS ILK AND THUS I KNOW WHERE THEY'VE TAKEN YOUR CRYSTAL...
LOOK THERE... HER EYES LIKE INK...

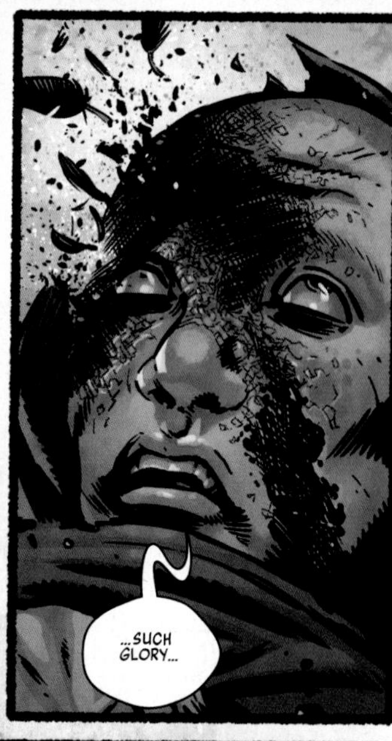
...SUCH GLORY...

...SHADIZAR.
A CITY OF WICKED WEALTH, BLOODY BOUNTY... AND MAGIC.
ROTTEN MAGIC.
THE CITY IS A DAY'S RIDE FROM HERE, IF WEATHER COOPERATES.
YOU--YOU'LL TAKE ME THERE?
I SAID WE'D GET THE SHARD, DIDN'T I? A CIMMERIAN FORGES HIS PROMISES LIKE STEEL.
LET'S GO.

THE WITCH'S MIND WANDERS BACK TO HER FRIENDS. THE NIGHTMARE OF THEIR DEMISE STILL LINGERS.
IF SHE COULD OPEN HER EYES AND SEE THE LIGHT, MAYBE IT WOULD FADE...
...BUT HER GAZE IS EVER DARK AND HER FUTURE EQUALLY UNCERTAIN.
THE BARBARIAN IS HARSH, UNYIELDING AND CLEARLY CARRIES A DARKNESS OF HIS OWN.
BUT SHE ALSO SENSES HE WOULD MARCH THROUGH THE GATES OF HELL ITSELF BEFORE LETTING ANY HARM BEFALL HER.
TRAVEL IS A BOND SHARED BETWEEN THE ROAD AND ITS PASSENGERS.
RELYING ON ONE ANOTHER... AND THE SOLACE OF THE SHARED EXPERIENCE.

SHADIZAR BECKONS, BUT WE'LL WAIT 'TIL NIGHT BEFORE WE ENTER.
WON'T THAT LOOK SUSPICIOUS?
I'M NOT WELCOME IN THE WICKED CITY, SO IT'S EITHER ENTERING UNDER COVER OF DARKNESS OR NOT AT ALL.
I SEE.

REST WHILE YOU CAN, WANDA. WE'LL NEED OUR SENSES SHARP TONIGHT.

WOULD THAT THE WITCH COULD REST AND BE AT PEACE.
BUT UNRESOLVED MATTERS STILL TWIST DEEP WITHIN HER MIND.

THE FEAR THAT SHE WOULD NEVER SEE HER FRIENDS OR LOVED ONES AGAIN.

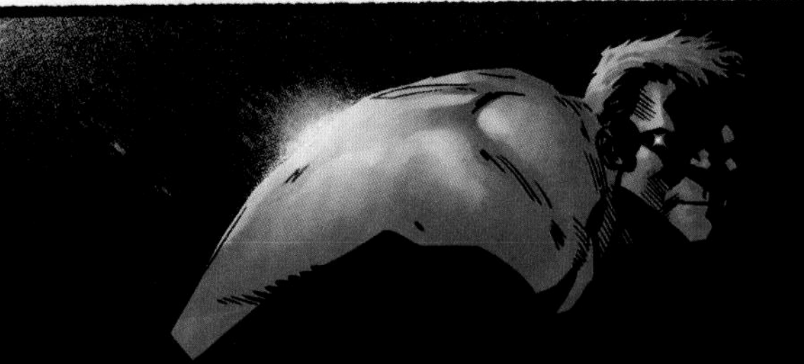
...AND THE RAGE...

CONAN SLUMBERS AS WELL.
IN HIS DREAM, HE IS AN ARCHER WALKING THROUGH THE RUINS OF A CASTLE MADE OF NIGHTMARES, IN A LAND MADE OF NIGHTMARES.

THERE IS A NIGHTMARE IN EVERY STICK...EVERY STONE.
THE NIGHTMARE IS ALL AROUND HIM...
OH.
GOD.
YOU MEAN HIM?

...AND THE NIGHTMARE HAS A FACE.
'CAUSE THAT GUY'S NOT THE GOD OF ANYTHING ANYMORE.

A DEMON'S FACE.
OR DID YOU MEAN ME?

YOU...YOU KILLED HIM. HYPNOS.
YOU JUST... SNAPPED HIS NECK...
YEAH, I SHOULD'VE HID IN A TREE AND SHOT HIM WITH AN ARROW WHILE HE WAS A 90-POUND SCIENTIST.
THAT'S HOW A REAL AVENGER DOES IT, RIGHT?
WHATEVER. SO SOMEBODY DIED AND LEFT A COOL MAGIC GEM BEHIND-- HAPPENS EVERY DAY.
HOW DO WE MAKE IT WORK? WOULD NIGHTMARE KNOW, OR--

I WOULD NOT.
GAAAH!

WHAT? THIS REALM IS MINE AGAIN. I'M ALWAYS JUST BEHIND YOU WHILE YOU SLEEP.
BUT AS FOR THIS BAUBLE...IT IS A POWER FOR THE WAKING WORLD. I ONLY KEPT IT AS A BARGAIN WITH ZEUS.
I FEAR THE KEY TO UNLOCKING IT DIED WITH HIM...

HNH. YOU'RE OVERTHINKING IT.
YOU DON'T UNTIE THE GORDIAN KNOT.
AND I DON'T BOTHER WITH KEYS.
HULK... JUST...
JUST THINK THIS THROUGH, OKAY? THINK ABOUT WHAT YOU'RE DOING...
OH, I'M THINKING, BARTON. I'M THINKING ABOUT ENDLESS NIGHT.
ENDLESS NIGHT AND THE END OF THE HUMAN WORLD.
KRK
KNOW WHAT I THINK ABOUT THAT?
KRR
K-K
KRAK

THERE IS A GOD WHO LIVES ON A GREAT MOUNTAIN.
HE IS GRIM AND SAVAGE AND HATES WEAKLINGS. IT IS USELESS TO ASK HIS AID, FOR HE BRINGS ONLY DOOM TO MANKIND.
AND IN HIS DREAM, CONAN KNOWS...THIS IS HIS CREATURE.
IT'S A GOOD PLACE TO START.
A CREATURE OF CROM.

BRUCE!
DEMON!
WHAT WAS THAT, WOMAN?!
DID YOU SEND THAT VISION INTO MY HEAD?!
NO!
I...I...
I'M SEEING ANOTHER SHARD... AND ITS POWER TAKEN TO FEED A MONSTER.
I SAW THAT MONSTER. HE IS STRENGTH INCARNATE.
ONE OF CROM'S OWN DOOMS, SET TO PUNISH MANKIND.
HAVE YOU ALWAYS SEEN SUCH THINGS FROM WORLDS BEYOND?
NO...THE DARK GODDESS WHO CURSED MY EYES CONNECTED ME TO THE PIECES OF HER BROKEN SOUL.
YOU HAVE ENDURED MUCH PAIN AND DEATH, HAVEN'T YOU?
YES.
IT IS THE WAY OF THINGS...

WE CAN'T.
BACK HOME, I...THERE'S SOMEONE...
I CAN'T.
NO. NOR COULD I.
IN MY HEART, I AM STILL...
...THERE WAS A PIRATE QUEEN NAMED BÊLIT.
SHE WAS MINE AND I HERS.
WE BUILT A LIFE OF PASSION AND PLUNDER SET AGAINST THE THUNDEROUS WAVES OF THE BLACK COAST.
AND THEN?
AND THEN DEATH, DESPAIR AND A LESSON.
NOTHING WILL LAST. ALL WILL BE FORGOTTEN...
...AND DARKNESS ALWAYS RETURNS.

BEHOLD SHADIZAR.
IN THE WRITINGS OF THE ANCIENT ZAMORAN SCRIBES, IT IS REFERRED TO AS "THE SHINING JEWEL UPON THE SANDS."
IT IS SAID THE ANCIENT ZAMORAN SCRIBES HAD A WELL-DEVELOPED SENSE OF HUMOR.
IT IS ALSO SAID THAT TO LIVE IN SHADIZAR, THE WICKED CITY, YOU MUST KEEP FOUR EYES IN YOUR HEAD--
--TWO IN FRONT AND TWO IN BACK--
=YAWN=
--AND NEVER CLOSE A ONE.
OW!
DAMNED DESERT WIND-- BLEW SAND IN MY EYES--
REALLY? YOURS AS WELL?
WHAT ARE THE ODDS OF THAT, EH?

WE'RE THROUGH THE GATES, THANKS TO YOUR SORCERY. BUT NOT OUT OF DANGER YET.
MY FACE IS WELL KNOWN TO THE NIGHT WORSHIPPERS...
IT'S NOT JUST THEM WE NEED TO WORRY ABOUT.

I TOLD YOU. MY ENEMY CAN SEE THROUGH MY EYES, AND SHE'S LOOKING FOR THE SHARD.
IF SHE SEES IT, SHE COMES TO GET IT. AND THEN WE DIE.

AS THEY ENTER THE MERCHANTS' QUARTER, CONAN SEARCHES THE SIGNS ABOVE THE STOREFRONTS FOR THE SYMBOLS OF A PARTICULAR TRADE.
HE LOOKS FOR THE MORTAR AND PESTLE... THE STAR-IN-CIRCLE... THE SIGN OF FIVE...
ale
UNLESS WE BLOCK HER VIEW...

...THE MARKS OF MAGIC.
TING
HO, MERCHANT. MY FRIEND IS UNDER A CURSE.
WE NEED SOMETHING TO HIDE HER FROM SORCEROUS SIGHT...
SAY NO MORE, FRIEND. I'VE AN ADEPT'S CLOAK WITH THE RIGHT PROPERTIES.
A FINE PIECE, THOUGH. HARD TO PART WITH...

...FOR LESS THAN FIFTY GOLD.

TEN.

TEN? YOU'RE MURDERING ME WHERE I STAND!
FORTY.

I WILL MURDER YOU WHERE YOU STAND.
FIFTEEN.

DO WE REALLY HAVE TIME FOR--

THIRTY-FIVE.
AND NOT A GROAT LOWER. UNDER TORTURE.

I KNOW SOME DARK TORTURES.
TWENTY.

THIRTY. FINAL OFFER, AND I MEAN THAT.
SPREAD MY ENTRAILS FOR THE CROW CULT, I'LL STILL NOT--

WAIT.
CROW CULT?

OH, YOU KNOW--THE NIGHT-GOD WORSHIPPERS. LOCAL RELIGION.
USED TO BE A BAT CULT, BUT THEN SOMEONE KILLED THE BAT.
SO, THIRTY IT IS?
FOR THE CLOAK AND INFORMATION--WHERE IN TOWN I MIGHT FIND THIS CROW CULT.
YOU SEEM LIKE A MAN WHO KNOWS SUCH THINGS...
OH, I DO--BUT IF YOU'RE WISE, YOU'LL STAY AWAY. I'D HATE TO SEND YOU BOTH OFF TO DIE.
ESPECIALLY IN AS FINE A CLOAK AS THIS ONE...
IT IS FINE. WHICH BIT HAS THE MAGIC IN IT?
SEE THE EDGING? EVERY RUNE ON THAT--HAND-STITCHED BY MASTER MAGES NORTH OF MESSANTIA.
IT'LL BLOCK OUT SCRYING POOLS, CRYSTAL BALLS, EVEN THE VISION OF THE--
--GODS.
RRRIPP

HERE.
TIE IT 'ROUND YOUR EYES.

...
THIRTY FOR THE CLOAK.
SENDING YOU TO DIE, I'LL THROW IN FOR FREE.

EVEN WITH THE MERCHANT'S INFORMATION, THEIR SEARCH TAKES THEM THROUGH THE NIGHT. SHADIZAR'S UNDERBELLY CONCEALED MORE THAN ONE SACRIFICIAL CHAMBER...AS THE CIMMERIAN LEARNED ALL TOO WELL OVER THE YEARS.
I HEAR VOICES AHEAD. I DON'T UNDERSTAND THE LANGUAGE.
STOP FOR A MOMENT AND I CAN PERFORM THE SAME TRANSLATION ENCHANTMENT I USED ON YOU--
DON'T BOTHER.
ALL THAT MATTERS IS THAT THEY BE STOPPED--AND QUICKLY, BEFORE THEIR CEREMONY TAKES THE LIFE OF A HELPLESS GIRL.
THIS IS NOT THE TIME FOR WORDS.

OH MA'KANNTA, GOD OF THE TALON--UNTO YOU, WE PRESENT THIS EBON KEY, THROBBING WITH ELDRITCH POWER!
TOO LONG HAVE THE BASTARD CHILDREN OF THE AKAH MA'AT BEEN FORCED TO HIDE!
WE BESEECH YOU TO PROTECT US FROM OUR ENEMIES AS WE RECLAIM THE SKIES OVER SHADIZAR! LET US PRAY!
THEY DO--WITH A SKULL-PIERCING ND THAT STRIKES LIKE A FIST TO SENSES.
ONE, THE WRETCHED AVIAN-WORSHIPPERS IT A DEAFENING SHRIEK--A CAW, A ENING REMINISCENT OF NOTHING HER THAN FLINT SCRAPING BONE.
DO THEY HAVE THE FRAGMENT? REMEMBER, YOU MUST RETRIEVE IT WITHOUT LETTING ME SEE IT, OR ELSE THE NIGHT QUEEN WILL HOME IN ON US IN AN INSTAN--
OH MY GOD! THAT SOUND!
AT LEAST THIS WAY THEY'LL NOT HEAR MY APPROACH OVER THEIR OWN CLATTER! STAY HERE!
BUT--
I'VE HAD ENOUGH ELDRITCH FILTH FOR ONE DAY! LET THIS BE DONE WITH SINEW AND STEEL!

MA'KANNTA, WITH THIS KEY WE UNLOCK THE PRISON THAT HAS SO UNJUSTLY KEPT YOU FROM US, YOUR FAITHFUL!
WE SUMMON THEE IN BLOOD AND--
SHUNK
NO!
THE SHARD MISSES THE MAIDEN'S HEART, BUT A CUT IS STILL MADE, SPILLING FORTH A SLIVER OF CRIMSON...
AS THE PRIEST'S ARM FALLS, HIS MAKESHIFT DAGGER PLUMMETS TOWARD HIS TERRIFIED VICTIM NONETHELESS.

UGH--
GH TO CRACK
AL AROUND
AN GOD!
NG OUT FROM SOME
ONIC REALM ALL BUT
OTTEN--THE DEIFIC
T SHRIEKS AND FANS
LAMES OF
EMONIUM!
RE IS NO
REAT. THERE
NLY COMBAT--
--AND THE METTLE OF
A WARRIOR-BORN!
AWAY WITH YOU, SHADOW OF DEATH!
AWAY WITH YOU ALL, GODS OR MONSTERS!
SURRENDER TO THE SAVAGE SWORD OF CONAN!

CONAN!
I MUST DO SOMETHING. EVEN IF I HAVE TO CAST BLINDLY--
HELP!
WHOEVER YOU ARE, PLEASE HELP! TH-THEY TRIED TO KILL ME! I HAVE TO GET AWAY!
PLEASE! I'LL PAY YOU!
I--I'LL TRY--
TAKE THIS! IT'S THEIR TREASURE!
THE WITCH BOUND HER EYES AGAINST MAGIC. BUT AT THE TOUCH OF THE SHARD CALLED THE NIGHT THAT IS UPON HER SKIN, WANDA'S STOMACH LURCHES--
NO!
--FOR THERE IS MORE THAN ONE WAY TO SEE.
HNNGH!

WHAT MADNESS--?
MA'KANNTAAAAA--
AIEEEE!
KK-KSSHHH
CONAN! THIS WAY!
WE HAVE TO RUN BEFORE IT'S--

TOO LATE.

PITIFUL SOULS. I'VE DONE THEM A FAVOR, FREEING THEM FROM THE MISGUIDED BURDEN OF WORSHIPPING ANYTHING BUT ME.
YOUR ALLIES PUT UP A FINE STRUGGLE, YOU SIMPERING SHREW...BUT FOR ALL THEIR SUPPOSED MIGHT, HERCULES AND HIS AVENGERS COULD NOT STOP ME.
WHAT CHANCE DO YOU TWO HAVE?

SPOTLIGHT ON CONAN THE BARBARIAN

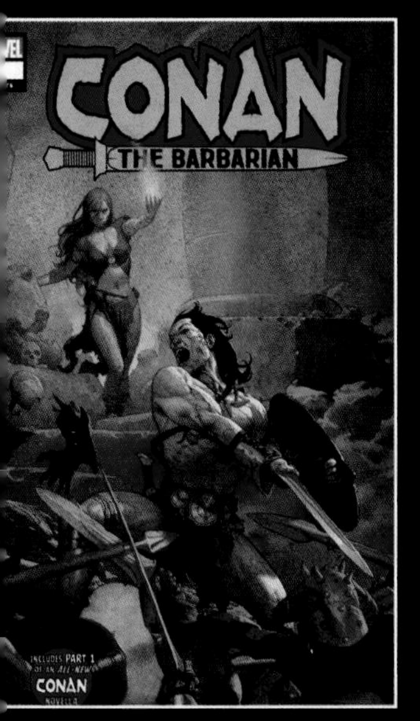

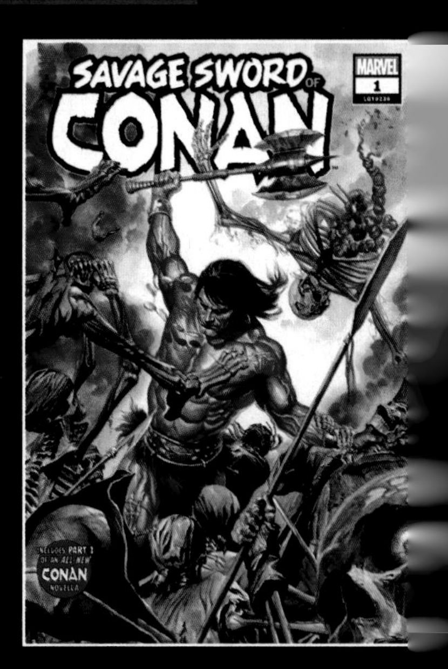

*ow, oh prince, that between the years when the oceans drank Atlantis and the gleaming
es, and the years of the rise of the Sons of Aryas, there was an age undreamed of, wher
ning kingdoms lay spread across the world like blue mantles beneath the stars...Hithe
ne Conan, the Cimmerian, black-haired, sullen-eyed, sword in hand, a thief, a reaver, a
yer, with gigantic melancholies and gigantic mirth, to tread the jeweled thrones of the
th under his sandaled feet."*

--The Nemedian Chronicles

he planning of AVENGERS: NO SURRENDER, we landed very quickly on the hook our third month--the Hulk had been killed in CIVIL WAR II, and this was the fect place to bring him back with a bang. As we went into AVENGERS: NO ROAD ME, one of our first questions was...what's our Hulk moment this time? What's bomb we can drop at the midway point that will reverberate across the entire rvel Universe?

e answer, we decided, was Conan the Barbarian.

bert E. Howard's savage Cimmerian burst onto the literary scene in the 1930s d would later enjoy a well-loved run of comics from Marvel from the '70s to the 0s. When we learned that Conan was making the trek back to the House of Ideas ound the time we were aiming to launch AVENGERS: NO ROAD HOME, the pieces fell into place.

s may be Conan's first foray into the modern Marvel Universe, but it won't be last. And if you'd like to learn more about Conan and his world as you wait to e his fate play out in AVENGERS: NO ROAD HOME, be sure to pick up CONAN THE RBARIAN, SAVAGE SWORD OF CONAN and AGE OF CONAN: BÊLIT, all on sale w!

Alanna

7

I DON'T SLEEP AT NIGHT ANY-MORE.
NO!
BUT I STILL HAVE DREAMS.
SHADIZAR.
BELIEVE THIS IS MINE.
COME TO ME, SHARD OF MY SOUL. TEACH ME HOW TO UNLOCK YOU.
TO TAKE BACK THE POWER ZEUS STOLE.
MENTAL PICTURES. VIVID THOUGHTS I CAN'T QUITE SHAKE OFF.
SOMETIMES I THINK ABOUT ALL THE LIGHT IN THE UNIVERSE. ALL THOSE RAYS AND WAVES AND PARTICLES, ALL ON THEIR INFINITE JOURNEYS.
BUT WHAT TO DO WITH YOU? FOR CAUSING ME SUCH TROUBLE?
SHALL I FEED OU TO OIZYS, MY YOUNGEST?
AND I WONDER IF THEY'RE LIKE ME.
OR GIVE YOU TO THE...
...TO THE...
IF THEY USED TO BE HUMAN.

TO THE TWINS...?
SEE, I USED TO BE HUMAN. BUT NOT ANYMORE.
I'M SENTIENT RADIATION.
ANYTHING ON THE ELECTROMAGNETIC SPECTRUM AND A FEW THINGS AROUND IT.
CONAN? WHAT'S HAPPENING?
I... DO NOT KNOW...
GAMMA RAYS. NEUTRINOS. ELECTRICITY.
VISIBLE LIGHT.
AND I CAN SHAPE THAT LIGHT. MAKE IT A HOLOGRAM OF ANYONE I'VE EVER SEEN. OR TWO ANYONES.

A SHELL OF LIVING LIGHT THAT DISGUISES MY FRIENDS AS MY ENEMIES...
...SO WELL THAT EVEN THEIR MOTHER WOULDN'T NOTICE.
WHAT... WHAT ARE YOU...?
ALL THAT, AND I'VE BEEN A LIGHT-BEING FOR...NOT EVEN A DECADE YET.
I'M MONICA RAMBEAU.
"SPECTRUM."
IF YOU'RE NASTY.
WHAT AM I GOING TO BE AT THE END OF A MILLENNIUM?

I NEVER USED TO WORRY ABOUT THAT. BUT NOW...WELL, HERE'S AN EXAMPLE.
IF I'D KNOWN NYX'S BIG ENTRANCE WOULD KILL ALL THESE DEATH CULTISTS, I'D HAVE MADE MY MOVE SOONER. TRIED TO PREVENT THAT.
BUT NOW THAT IT'S HAPPENED? I'M WAITING.
FOR THE RIGHT MOMENT TO AVENGE THEM.
BUT IF YOU LIVE-- THEN--WHA ABOUT--
WAITING FOR HER TO REALIZE...
--MY CHILDREN--
...WHAT SHE DID WHEN SHE THOUGHT SHE WAS KILLING MY FRIENDS.
NO!
DEMON-- I WILL DESTROY YOU! YOU--YOU MADE ME--
SO SHE ATTACKS ANGER--WITHOU THINKING--AND LEA HERSELF OPEN.
A MOTHER'S PA AND I'VE TURN IT INTO STRATE
I DIDN'T MAKE YOU DO ANYTHING.
SOMETIMES I DON'T LIKE HOW HARD I'VE BECOME.

AND YOU BROUGHT THIS ON YOURSELF!
I'VE BEEN THINKING ABOUT THIS--A POTENTIAL MAGIC BULLET.
IF I BLEND ULTRAVIOLET, VISIBLE AND INFRARED LIGHT--I CAN MATCH THE SUN'S OUTPUT EXACTLY--
--TO BECOME THE LIGHT OF DAY.
SUNLIGHT?
YOU USE SUNLIGHT AGAINST ME?
FOOLISH CHILD--I AM NOT SOME VAMPIRE WHO WILTS AT THE LIGHT OF A SINGLE STAR!
THE NIGHT HOLDS A THOUSAND STARS--AND THE MOON IN THEIR MIDST--
--THAT REFLECTS THE LIGHT--AND LESSENS IT!
UNNH--
THE MOON AS HER SHIELD.
DAMMIT--I'VE SPENT THE LAST FEW YEARS FIGHTING COSMIC THREATS--
--THE BEYOND CORPORATION, SPACE GODS ARMED WITH SCIENCE BEYOND SCIENCE--
--BUT THIS IS MAGIC, NOT SCIENCE.
MONICA--
HER GAMBIT FAILED--WE MUST NOT!
INTO THE FRAY!
AND THAT MEANS I DON'T KNOW THE RULES...

THE NIGHTMARE REALM.
...IF THERE EVEN ARE ANY.
WELL, NOW. THIS HAS BEEN FUN.
BUT I DON'T ENJOY HAVING GUESTS OVER--I PREFER VICTIMS. SO IT'S TIME YOU ALL LEFT.
WITH MY POWER RESTORED, I CAN OPEN A PORTAL ANYWHERE IN THE WAKING WORLD. I CAN PUT YOU WHERE YOU NEED TO BE.
AND IN RETURN--MY DEBT TO YOU IS CANCELED. YES?
GROOVY. PUT US INSIDE THE VAULT AT GRNAX'S GAMBLING PALACE ON SATYRICON VI.
I'LL CUT THE ALARMS FROM THE INSIDE--THEN FOR THE GETAWAY, WE JUST NEED PLIERS, A LITTLE HYDROGEN SULFIDE AND A PAIR OF FAKE EARS--
YOU CAN ROB CASINOS ON YOUR OWN TIME, ROCKET.
WE NEED TO FIND WANDA AND THE OTHERS--SO WHEREVER THEY'VE GONE, THAT'S WHERE WE'RE--
EUPHORIA.
HUH?

IT'S A SENTIENT WORLD.
TREATS EVERYONE REAL NICE--MAKES THEIR DREAMS COME TRUE. FUN PLACE TO VISIT, RIGHT?
ANY OBJECTIONS?

OU...WANT TO GO ON ACATION?
NOW?
EHH, I COULD TAKE A BREAK. IT'S BEEN A TOUGH COUPLE DAYS, Y'KNOW?
ANYWHERE THAT AIN'T A NIGHTMARE DIMENSION WOULD BE GREAT, IF I'M HONEST...

LOOKS LIKE YOU'RE OUTVOTED, MR. BARTON. EUPHORIA IT IS--SOUNDS GHASTLY.
OFF YOU GO...
UNBELIEVABLE.
YOU KNOW WHAT? FINE. COUNT ME IN.

BECAUSE I DON'T KNOW HOW YOU KNOW ABOUT THIS EUPHORIA PLACE, BUT I DO KNOW THAT LOOK. YOU'VE GOT PLANS.
AND WHEN I FIND OUT WHAT THEY ARE?
I WON'T NEED A SPECIAL GAMMA ARROW TO PUT YOU DOWN.

HNH.
SEE, WE'RE HAVING FUN ALREADY.
THIS IS GETTING SERIOUS.

ANY HOPE WE HAD OF KEEPING THIS FIGHT QUICK AND CONTAINED, USING SPEED AND SURPRISE TO OUR ADVANTAGE...
...IT'S LONG GONE NOW.
WHEN GODS BATTLE, IT'S ALWAYS A MESS.
KRAKOOOOM
DON'T WORRY, WANDA-- I'VE GOT YOU!
MONICA?! I HEARD YOUR VOICE, BUT DIDN'T KNOW WHAT WAS HAPPENING...
SHE'S STILL BLIND.
ARE THE OTHERS WITH YOU?
IS VIZH OKAY?
HE'S STILL TICKING, IF THAT'S WHAT YOU MEAN. WE'RE ALL A BIT CRISPY AROUND THE EDGES RIGHT NOW.
THAT QUIVER IN HER VOICE AS SHE ASKS ABOUT VISION...
WHATEVER THEI CURRENT SITUATI THERE'S STILL SOMETHING THE

NDA'S BEEN THROUGH MUCH AND I WASN'T THERE TO HELP HER WITH ANY OF IT.
I NEED YOU TO AY HERE, HILE I--
NO! I'M NOT WAITING AROUND WHILE YOU FIGHT!
SHE'S BRISTLING WITH ANGER. IN THE PAST I WOULD'VE FELT GUILTY... FOR NOT LISTENING TO HER...
I'M AN AVENGER, MONICA! DON'T SIDELINE ME!
NOW, LEAVING HER HERE IS JUST... STRATEGY.
WE CAN'T RISK IT.
NO!
IS THAT US GROWING APART? OR THE FIRST SIGN OF SOMETHING WORSE?
OVER A THOUSAND YEARS, WHO ELSE WILL I GROW APART FROM? EVERYONE? MYSELF? IS THAT JUST WHAT HAPPENS?
HERCULES IS IMMORTAL, TOO.
BUT HIS HUMANITY IS THE STUFF OF LEGEND.
THOOM
BLOOD WILL BE PAID FOR WHAT YOU'VE DONE, NIGHT WITCH!

SO IS IT JUST ME?
I WILL NOT YIELD UNTIL-- RRK!
IN TIMES PAST, I BELIEVED PHYSICAL CONFRONTATION WAS BENEATH ME.
BUT I WAS WRONG, HALF-GOD.
SLAYING ZEUS WAS A VISCERAL THRILL.
AND KILLING YOU WILL BE JUST AS--
NNNN--!
N'GAAH!
WANDA?
I'M NOT HELPLESS, DAMMIT...
WELL CAUGHT, SPECTRUM!
SWING BACK 'ROUND AND LAUNCH ME TOWARD THE NIGHT QUEEN, SO I MAY PUMMEL HER INTO DARK DUST!

SY-
Y-SYSTEM
NSTABLE.
PHASE
CY-CY-CYCLE
INTERMITTENT.
FI-GDRRYYY-
Y-Y-Y-Y-Y--
NON-C-C-
COMBATANTS--
PINNED UND-D-
D-D-DER THE
RUBBLE.
SUGGESTED
C-C-COURSE
OF ACTION--CUT
AND CLEAR DEBRIS
IN S-S-
SECTIONS--
A
MONSTER!
STAY
AWAY!
DO--DO--
DO NOT BE AF-
F-F-RAID.
"O THOU MONSTER
IGNORANCE, HOW
DEFORMED DOST
THOU LOOK..."
WHAT IN
HELL'S NAME
ARE YOU?!
EH?

MAYBE I AM GROWING APART FROM EVERYONE.
SOME KIND OF STEEL DEVIL?
WHATEVER YOU ARE, YOU'LL GO NO FARTHER!
MAYBE I'M LOSING WHAT HUMAN IS.
S-S-S-S- SAVE THEM--
P-P- PLEASE.
BUT I'VE GOT A WAY TO GO YET...
RRRR--!

...BECAUSE I'M NOT THIS IDIOT.
WHAT THE HELL DID YOU DO?!
WITCHES, GOLEMS AND NOW SPIRITS!
ARE THERE ANY HERE THAT CAN BE WOUNDED BY A MAN'S BLADE? IS IT ONLY THOSE I LOVED WHO CAN DIE?
BÊLIT LIES IN HER GRAVE-- AND YOU WIZARD'S SPAWN MAKE A MOCKERY OF US ALL--
THAT'S ENOUGH. SEE THAT UP THERE? SHE'S YOUR TARGET!
AND IF WE DON'T STOP HER, WE WILL ALL DIE!
VIZH, I'M JUICING UP YOUR ARRAYS WITH PURE SOLAR ENERGY. CAN YOU INITIATE A SELF-REPAIR?
I WILL T-TRY...
FORGIVE ME, SPIRIT. THERE...THERE IS GRIEF IN MY HEART.
A WEAKNESS THAT MAKES THE WHOLE WORLD SEEM MY FOE...
"WOULD I HAD MET MY DEAREST FOE IN HEAVEN OR EVER I HAD SEEN THAT DAY..."
TREATING WANDA LIKE GLASS WHILE KING MACHO RUNS AMOK-- MY LEADERSHIP SKILLS ARE DEFINITELY RUSTY.
BUT GETTING NYX ANGRY WAS A GOOD MOVE. KEEPS HER FOCUSED ON US-- NOT THE SHARD.
OF COURSE, THAT ANGER COULD ALSO GET US KILLED--

--OR WORSE.
KRRK
THE SECOND THE SHARD CRACKS, IT HITS ME.
OF COURSE.
THE SHARD'S A CONTAINER FOR THE POWER INSIDE.
WHOEVER DESTROYS THE SHARD--BREAKS OPEN THE CONTAINER--
--THEY GET THE POWER.
BUT I SAW IT A SECOND AFTER SH
DID--BECAUSE DESP
EVERYTHING--
--I STILL REACT LIKE A PERSON--
VOYAGER!
--AND SHE REACTS LIKE A GOD.
HELL OF A W
TO LEARN T
DIFFERENC

THIS...FEELS... MAGNIFICENT!
IT STEELS ME! IT RESTORES MY SENSES! IT BINDS ME TO THE OTHER FRAGMENTS! IT--
--IT--

WHAT IS IT? WHAT DID YOU SEE?
YOU'LL NEVER KNOW.
AAAAAAAAAAAAAAGGH!
YOU'RE ONLY HUMAN.

NO MORE NEED FOR YOU. I'LL FIND MY OWN WAY FROM HERE.
THWAM

NO NEED FOR LOOSE ENDS, EITHER.
AVENGERS--

HNNGH!

YOU STILL HAVE A BIT OF MY MAGIC IN YOU, DON'T YOU?

I'LL TAKE THAT BACK.
EYAAAAAHH!

BE A GOOD GIRL.
CLEAN UP FOR MOTHER WHILE SHE RUNS HER NEXT ERRAND.
WITH PLEASURE
WITH PLEASURE
WITH PLEASURE
SZZZAKKK
MONICA!
HELP...
...HELP VOYAGE
WANDA, ARE YOU HURT?
IT WAS AGONY FOR A MOMENT, BUT-- BUT I'M BETTER.
I'M NO LONGER BLIND--
--THOUGH I'M NOT SURE THAT'S A BLESSING!
OIZYS--

-SHE'S
DING OFF
NOCENT
EOPLE!
AND FROM THEIR DESPAIR...
FROM THEIR DESPAIR...
FROM THEIR DESPAIR...
...A CHAMPION.
AMPION.
...A CHAMPION.
WHAT FORM OF CHAMPI--
ENOUGH!
WHATEVER MISBEGOTTEN MONSTER YOU CHOOSE TO HIDE BEHIND--
--I SWEAR BY CROM THAT I SHALL STRIKE IT DEAD!
AH YES, THE DEAD...
THE DEAD...
THE DEAD...

ONE OF THE DEAD CALLS OUT FOR YOUR BLOOD!
YOUR BLOOD!
YOUR BLOOD!
BÊLIT...?

'E ASSEMBLY

ey there, True Believers, and welcome back to the ASSEMBLY! This week, we've t a special look at how our two different art teams put their pages together, from pencils to color! Enjoy!

encils by **Paco Medina**

Inks by **Juan Vlasco**

Colors by **Jesus Aburtov**

Layouts and Inks by **Sean Izaakse**

Colors by **Marcio Menyz**

8

SHADIZAR.
CONAN!
HEN I WAS A YEAR OLD, I
EW ASSASSINS SENT BY
HE QUEEN OF THE GODS--
MY STEPMOTHER. THOSE
WERE THE FIRST LIVES
I TOOK.
AND TO MY SHAME, NOT THE LAST.
I HAVE KNOWN RAGE IN MY TIME. I HAVE SOUGHT REVENGE AND FOUND TRAGEDY. IN THIS LONG LIFE OF MINE, I HAVE KNOWN DARK DAYS.
I AM HERCULES PANHELLENIOS, THE PRINCE OF POWER...AND THIS DAY IS PERHAPS THE DARKEST OF ALL.

HE PLANET
UPHORIA.
I'M THE TRONGEST THERE IS.
YOU WON'T LIKE ME WHEN I'M ANGRY. OR WHEN I'M NOT.
THEY CALL ME THE HULK...AND THE NIGHT IS MY TIME.
HULK--DID YOU KNOW SHE WAS GOING TO BE HERE...?
THIS WAS SUPPOSED TO BE A VACATION, DAMMIT!

PROMISES WERE MADE!

DRINK IT IN, BARBARIAN...
DRINK IT IN, BARBARIAN...
IT IN, BARBARIAN...
...A WINE FERMENTED FROM YOUR DEEPEST SORROWS.
...A WINE FERMENTED FROM YOUR DEEPEST SORROWS.
...A WINE FERMENTED FROM YOUR DEEPEST SORROWS.
BÊLIT, MY LOVE...

SO LET ME HANDLE IT.
I'VE GOT A PLAN.
AND THIS IS NYX. GODDESS OF NIGHT.
WE WANT THE SAME THING--A CRYSTAL SHARD WITH A THIRD OF HER FULL POWER IN IT.
I GOT ONE ALREADY. USED IT TO FIND ITS BROTHER--SOMEWHERE ON THIS PLANET. LOOKS LIKE SHE DID THE SAME.
AND WHOEVER GETS THAT ONE--THE LAST SHARD OF NIGHT--GETS TO BE THE ONE TO END THE WORLD.

DARK WITH THE STAIN OF DEATH.
DARK WITH THE SCARS OF REGRET.
THE QUEEN OF NIGHT AND HER FOUL CHILDREN ARE STEALING AWAY THE LIGHT IN THE UNIVERSE AND THE LIGHT WITHIN OUR VERY SOULS...

A LIFE OF VIOLENCE DIGS WELLS OF ANGUISH DEEPER THAN WE CAN ADMIT TO OURSELVES.
WE SAILED ON AZURE WATERS AND BIT DEEP INTO THE FRUIT OF THE WORLD.
A SEARING PAIN WE DO NOT KNOW HOW TO CONFRONT.
THE QUEEN OF THE BLACK COAST AND HER FAITHFUL LION.
YES
ZAAAK
GRAAAH!
STOP-- OI-OI-OI-OIZYS.
HOLD ON, CONAN!

KNOW NOT WHO THIS WARRIOR IS, BUT HIS EXPRESSION TELLS ME MUCH ABOUT THE LIFE HE'S LED.
YOU...
I HAVE BEEN THAT BARBARIAN.
I HAVE FELT THE FRENZY OF ENDLESS ANGER.
YOU!
N'GAAAH!
EACH BATTLE BUILDS THE CALLUS AROUND ONE'S HEART.
TASTE MY BLADE, DOG!
SLASH
EACH DEATH BREEDS A SELF-FULFILLING PROPHECY.

AH, GEEZ.
THIS AIN'T MY IDEA OF PARADISE, BOYS.
MY. MORE LOST LAMBS.
YOU HAVE SOMETHING THAT IS MINE. I DON'T MUCH CARE FOR THAT.

A GOOD FIGHT IS PARADISE. YOU WANT YOUR OWN, GO FIND IT.
RUN?
LIVE.
I DON'T WANT THE RACCOON SKINNED-- AND YOU'RE JUST USELESS, BARTON. SO GO.

HE HAS A POINT.
SHUT UP AND HELP ME MAKE A BOW.

I'VE NEVER RUN FROM FIGHT IN MY LIFE. I C GIVE YOU THE NAMES A NUMBERS OF TWO DOZ DOCTORS AND SURGEONS WHO'LL BACK THAT UP.

"THIS WOMAN SNUFFED OUT EVERY SUN IN THE UNIVERSE.
"AT BEST, THERE ARE ENTIRE PLANETS THAT THINK THEIR GODS HAVE ABANDONED THEM.

"AT WORST, IT'S JUST A MATTER OF TIME BEFORE EVERYTHING WE'VE EVER KNOWN FREEZES TO DEATH."

LET'S GO!
IT'S "AVENGERS ASSEMBLE," NOT "AVENGERS, TAKE FIVE."

HNH. HOW ABOUT THAT.
NOT SO PUNY AFTER ALL...

THE BARBARIAN REFUSES TO SUCCUMB TO HIS WOUNDS.
YOUR MAGICS...DO NOT IMPRESS ME.
HEAL =KOFF= HEAL ME AND...I'LL GRANT YOU THE MERCY OF A SWIFT END.
POOR YOU.
YOU.
YOU.
FEED ME WITH YOUR DESPAIR...
FEED ME WITH YOUR DESPAIR...
FEED ME WITH YOUR DESPAIR...
...SO THAT I MAY WEAPONIZE IT.
...SO T I MAY APONIZE IT.
...SO T I MAY EAPONIZE IT.
WHAT'S HAPPENING? SHE LOOKS LIKE SHE'S ABOUT TO--
KZZKKT TZZZKK
WOULD THAT THE REST OF US HAD HIS STRENGTH.
NGGGH!
AAAAH!

JERICHO... MY LOVE...
JERICHO!
WHAT'S LEFT?
AFTER A THOUSAND YEARS, A MILLION YEARS...
...WHAT'S LEFT OF EVERYTHING I KNEW?
WHAT'S LEFT OF ME?
NO NO NO NO NO...
VIVIAN VISION
Loving Daughter
Taken Too Soon

WHAT'S *IN* THESE ARROWS, ANYWAY?
ONE'S CARRYIN' AN ANTIMATTER CHARGE CAPABLE O' BLOWIN' A HOLE IN A *KREE STAR CRUISER.*
THE OTHER'S JUST REAL SHARP.
DUC

AND WHAT ARE *EITHER* OF THEM SUPPOSED TO DO TO *ME?*

GET YOUR *ATTENTION*

THWOOM
LIKE SWATTING A *FLY*. MY POWER *AND* HERS--I'VE *NEVER* BEEN THIS STRONG.
THIS IS *TOO EASY.*

NICE THROW.
WHAT'RE YOU LOOKIN' FOR, BARTON?
WE COULD USE SOME GOLIATH-SIZED MUSCLES. I'M TRYING TO FIND THAT VIAL OF PYM PARTICLES I HAD. ONE LAST DOSE OF SIZE-CHANGING.
DO THEY NLY WORK ON MANS? COULD THEY MAYBE SHRINK HER AWAY?
FIRST ANSWER'S "NO," SECOND IS "I DOUBT IT." I--
LOOK OUT!
NOW SHE'S SERIOUS. NO MORE SNEERING. NO MORE BIG TALK.
SHE'S HITTING US WITH EVERYTHING SHE HAS.
GOOD.

OIZYS' POISON ENTERS MY SOUL, AND MY ***LEGS*** GIVE WAY. ALL I FEEL IS ***NOTHING***.
A WASTELAND INSIDE ME.
THE ***RAGE*** AT MY FAMILY'S DEATH...IT KEPT ME ***FIGHTING***. IT WAS ALL I HAD ***LEFT***.
NOW IT'S COLD, BITTE ***ASH***. WHAT ***GOOD*** IS IT
WHAT GOOD AM ***I?*** HERCULES THE ***JOKE***...ALWAYS THE ***FOOL***, SMILING LIKE AN IDIOT...
WHAT AM I ***FOR?***
I AM SO... ***TIRED***...ALWAYS SO TIRED...JUST...
JUST LET IT ***END***. LET THE GRAND TALES OF HERCULES AND HIS LABORS END HERE.

LET IT ***ALL*** END.
LET IT...

...
SOMEONE'S CRYING.

IT'S VOYAGER.
TOO WEAK... LET THIS HAPPEN... THEY ALL HATE ME, THEY HAVE TO...
SO ALONE... NO FAMILY, NO FATHER--STUPID, STUPID, STUPID--

OIZYS SEES ME SEE HER. AND LASHES OUT.
ORE PSYCHIC STINGS. MORE REMINDERS OF AIN...OLD HURTS AND HATES, SO MANY...

I WANT TO COLLAPSE. I WANT TO DRINK.
BUT I CAN'T.

THERE'S SOMETHING I HAVE TO DO.
A LABOR TO COMPLETE.
VOYAGER... YOU...

...YOU ARE NOT ALONE.
PLEASE. IF I CAN.

I'D LIKE TO HELP.

I SAID I HAD A **PLAN**.
HERE IT IS.
HIT HER.
HARD AS I CAN--A KILLING BLOW. **NOW**.
BECAUSE IF I GIVE HER **ONE MORE SECOND** TO **THINK...**
YOU HOLD A PORTION OF MY **POWER**, NIGHT CREATURE.
THAT GIVE YOU ADDE **STRENGT**
...BUT **CONTROL** IS ANOTHER MATTER.
HELL.
WHAT I WAS AFRAID OF.
GOD **GIVETH...**
FOR YO AND YO **ALONE**

--I RESCIND MY GIFT OF NIGHT.
AAARRRHHH!
...AND GOD TAKETH AWAY.
CAN'T STOP IT. STRONGEST THERE IS AND I STILL CAN'T STOP THE CHANGE.
AND BANNER--
--BANNER CAN'T HOLD THE POWER.
HELL.
I'M IN HELL.
THE HELL OF DAYLIGHT.
BECAUSE THE NIGHT IS MY TIME.

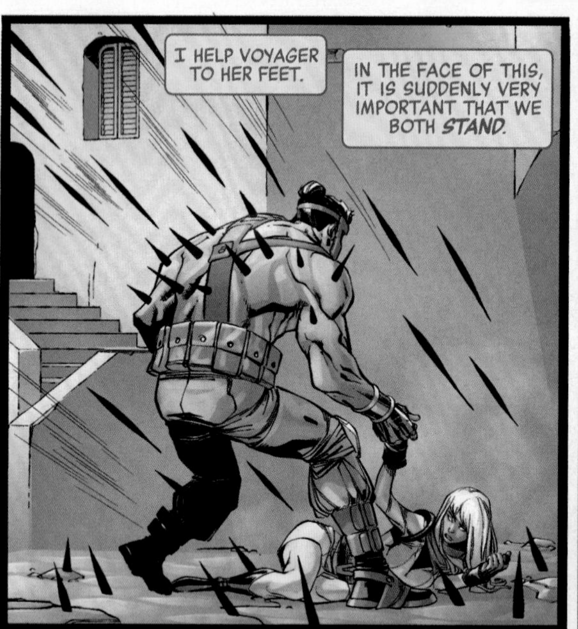
I HELP VOYAGER TO HER FEET.
IN THE FACE OF THIS, IT IS SUDDENLY VERY IMPORTANT THAT WE BOTH STAND.

AND THEN I TURN. AND I LOOK AT OIZYS, WHO IS MISERY.
SHE HAS SUCH VAST POWER OVER US. BU SOMETIMES...WHEN WE LOOK AT HER...

...WE CAN SEE HER CLEARLY.
YOU--YOU ARE SMALL AND WEAK--
AND WEAK--
AND WEAK--

AND SUDDENLY I KNOW WHAT I AM FOR.
NOT FOR VENGEANCE. NOT TO BE A CREATURE OF RAGE. I'M STRONGER THAN THAT.

MY PURPOSE IS TO FIND THE MISERY IN THIS LIFE...TO FIND DESPAIR, WHEREVER IT MIGHT HIDE...AND, AS BEST I CAN...
LISTEN TO ME--
TO ME--
TO ME--

...TO CRUSH IT.

AND THEN...TO SMILE LIKE AN IDIOT.
I'M NOT SURE HOW MUCH THAT HELPED. BUT I FEEL BETTER.
HOW ABOUT YOU?
SHE...SHE WAS IN MY HEAD FOR SO LONG...IT'S...
I DON'T KNOW IF I CAN FEEL BETTER. NOT RIGHT AWAY. BUT...I CAN THINK NOW.
AND I CAN FIGHT.
AYE. MY ONE REGRET IS THAT I DIDN'T PUT THE LIZARD TO THE SWORD MYSELF.
INSTEAD, I WILL TAKE MY VENGEANCE ON SHE WHO BORE THE BEAST--IF YOU'LL HAVE ME AT YOUR SIDE.
AND PERHAPS ONCE THE QUEEN OF NIGHT LIES DEAD...BÊLIT'S GHOST WILL REST IN MY MIND...
VENGEANCE WILL NOT CURE THAT PAIN, MY FRIEND. I KNOW.
BUT YOU CAN HELP US STOP THE NIGHT-GODDESS BEFORE SHE HURTS ANYONE ELSE.
VOYAGER--WITH YOUR POWERS, CAN YOU SEE WHERE SHE WENT?
I--I THINK SO. EVEN WITH OIZYS DEAD, THERE'S ENOUGH CONNECTION TO DIVINE HER LOCATION...BUT...

"...WE MUST HURRY."
MUCH BETTER.
THAT'S THE BEAUTY OF THESE FRAGMENTS. THEY'RE NOT ADDITIVE--THEY'RE EXPONENTIAL. I FEEL--
?
THAT HOUSE AGAIN. WHAT IS IT?
WHERE IS IT?
AND HOW CAN IT HAVE LIGHT...?

LEAD ME.
HOLD!
NYX! HALT!!!
ACROSS THE UNIVERSE... PLANET CALLED EUPHORIA...
IT TOOK... ALL MY STRENGTH...
I SHOUT BEFORE I REALIZE WE'RE TOO LATE TO STOP HER.
NYX HAS HER SECOND FRAGMENT.
THE NEXT MOVE IS HERS.
MORTALS.
DESPITE YOUR BEST EFFORTS, I'VE BEEN ABLE TO DEFEAT YOU IN YOUR REALM.

IMAGINE WHAT I'LL BE ABLE TO DO TO YOU IN MINE.
T-THE STARS--
ALL--ALL THE BILLIONS OF STARS--
OURANOS' EYES. THEY'RE...
THEY'RE GOING OUT.

WHAT IS EUPHORIA?

Omnipotence City, Shadizar and the Nightmare Realm, the
S: NO ROAD HOME road trip has some rich Marvel history th
might remember! Euphoria the living planet first appeared in SI
haven for Galactus survivors, providing everything its inhab
and happy...but Euphoria hasn't always proven adept at kno
itants need to be lulled into a peaceful stupor, or jolted into a

Does this latest locale spell relief for our heroes, or doom?
Read on and find out, True Believers!

9

EW YORK.
AMERICA, LIGHTNING--YOU'RE TH ME! THIS BLACKOUT'S EATING GLOBAL PANIC--BUT BETWEEN US, WE CAN BE EVERYWHERE AT ONCE!
TONI, WASP--YOUR JOB IS TO GET THE POWER BACK ON! ANY WAY YOU CAN!
GOMI, BILL THE LOBSTER, POD-2--EARTH'S TRIGGER FINGERS ARE GETTING ITCHY! YOUR ASSIGNMENT--PREVENT WORLD WAR III!
READY FOR THE FIRST G.I.R.L./R.E.S.C.U.E. JOINT MISSION, NADIA?
I AM IF YOU ARE!
EVERYTHING IS COOL.
T'CHALLA--CAN YOUR AVENGERS SQUAD HANDLE THE VAMPIRE PROBLEM?
IF YOU CAN HANDLE YOUR END, BLUE MARVEL--
I'M COMMANDING A WORLDWIDE FORCE OF INTERNATIONAL HEROES, PANTHER--THAT'LL HAVE TO BE ENOUGH!
AVENGERS WORLD--ASSEMBLE!
I ALWAYS THOUGHT THAT WHEN THE TIME CAME...HERCULES COULD BE THE HERO.

EUPHORIA.
INSTEAD, I FIND MYSELF IN DARKNESS, SHAKEN AND GRIEVING. READYING FOR FINAL BATTLE.
AND THEN I HEAR A VOICE.
ENOUGH.
A KIND VOICE.
WHO--
I AM EUPHORIA. I AM THIS PLANET.
FOR COUNTLESS MILLENNIA, I HAVE EXISTED ONLY TO MAKE MY DENIZENS... HAPPY.
TO FULFILL
THEN YOU POSSESS THE FINAL SHARD OF MY POWER--
YOU ALL DESIRE THAT.
AND YOUR WARRING THREATENS TO DISRUPT MY PARADISE.
SO I WONDER...CAN A DECISION BE MADE?
WHO NEEDS IT MOST?
I DO!
MY LADY-- FOR THE GOOD OF THE UNIVERSE, WE MUST HAVE THE--
I CANNOT SPEAK OF UNIVERSES. AM ONLY PLANET.
WHAT I
YOUR
GODLIN
WHAT IS IT
WANT?

HE SHARD. WE
ST HAVE THE
SHARD.
TO...TO DEFEAT
ENDLESS
NIGHT...

NOT THE GOAL OF SOME MISSION. THE ACHE OF YOUR HEART.
THE TRUTH.
WHAT DO YOU WANT?

...
RECENTLY, I TRIED TO MEND MY WAYS. MEND MY REPUTATION.

ANTED TO BE SEEN
S A LEGENDARY
HERO AGAIN.
SO I STOPPED DRINKING, AND THAT WAS HARD. BUT TO STOP BOASTING...

...THAT BECAME TOO HARD.
I WANTED TO BE SEEN AS THE LEGEND, YOU SEE. THE LEGEND PEOPLE WANTED.

I SWUNG BETWEEN PLAYING THE SERIOUS MAN, ACHING TO PROVE SOMETHING...
...AND PLAYING THE JESTER. EVERYONE'S FUNNY FRIEND.

I CAN'T BE
OSE PEOPLE
ANYMORE.
I CAN'T.
I WANT TO BE... WHO I WANT TO BE. AND THE MAN I WANT TO BE...

...HE DOES NOT BOAST. OR HAVE THINGS TO PROVE.
HE ONLY HELPS.

THAT'S ALL I WANT. ALL THAT MATTERS.
JUST TO HAVE HELPED SOMEONE.

I SEE.
AND WHAT DO YOU WANT, ARCHER?
ME? I DON'T KNOW, I WANT TO HEAR MUSIC THE WAY I USED TO, I GUESS...BEFORE MY HEARING WAS DAMAGED.
I WANT TO BE 20 AGAIN...I WANT...
AND WHAT DO YOU WANT, IMMORTAL?

...I WANT A SHOT. ONE PERFECT SHOT.
ONE GOOD ARROW.

WE NEED LIGHT. WE CAN'T LIVE WITHOUT IT. I CAN'T LEAD WITHOUT IT.
I...I WANT TO BE THAT LIGHT.

BUT...NOT FOREVER
I KNOW THAT NO

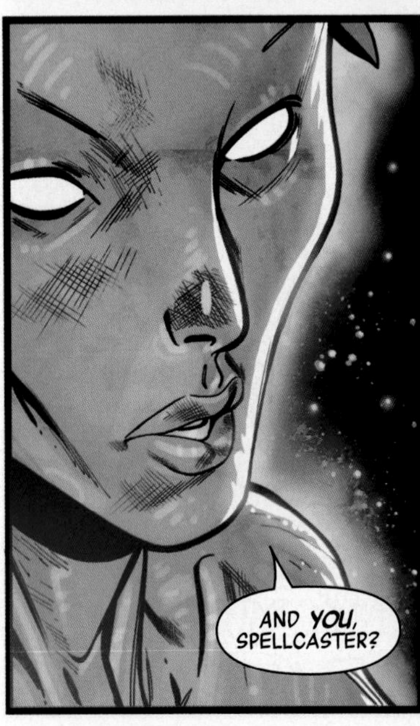

AND YOU, SPELLCASTER?

I CAN SEE AGAIN--BUT IN THIS DARK, I MIGHT AS WELL BE BLIND.
I NEED TO SEE--

--TO SEE HER FACE.
WHEN I TAKE A WITCH'S VENGEANCE FOR ALL SHE'S DONE!

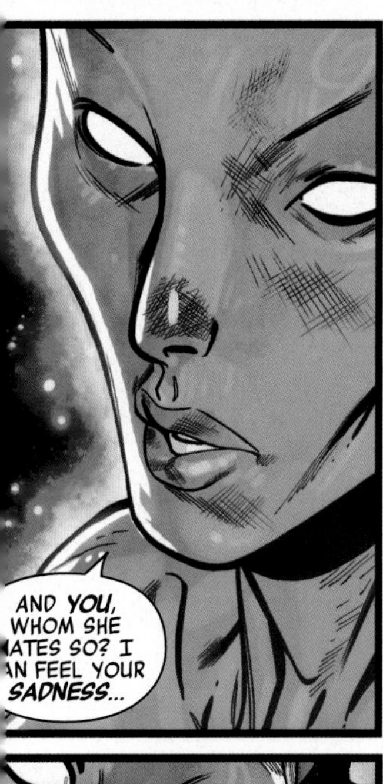
AND YOU, WHOM SHE ATES SO? I AN FEEL YOUR SADNESS...

I WANT THE SAME.
ONCE... ONCE I WOULD HAVE ASKED FOR ACCEPTANCE. RESPECT. A HOME.

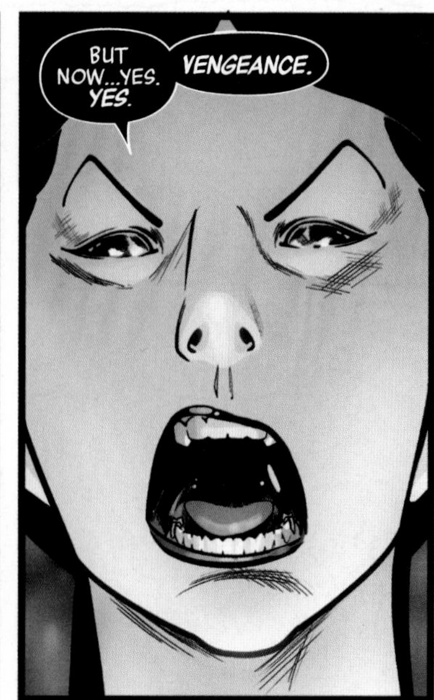
BUT NOW...YES. YES.
VENGEANCE.

AND YOU?
YOU WHOSE SADNESS DWARFS ALL HERE?

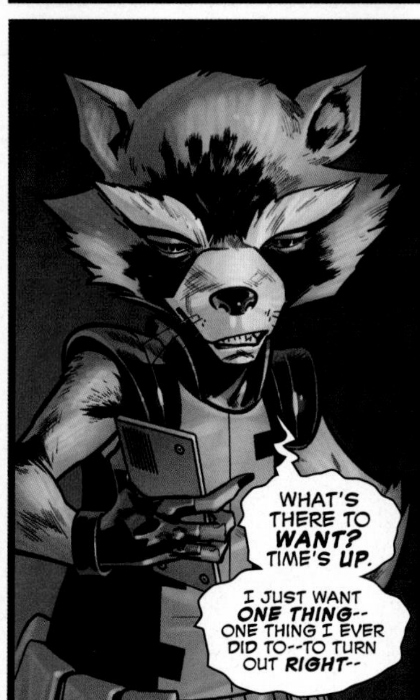
WHAT'S THERE TO WANT? TIME'S UP.
I JUST WANT ONE THING-- ONE THING I EVER DID TO--TO TURN OUT RIGHT--

HUH. WEIRD.
FORGOT I STOLE THIS.

AND YOU?
DO YOU HAVE WANTS? DESIRES?

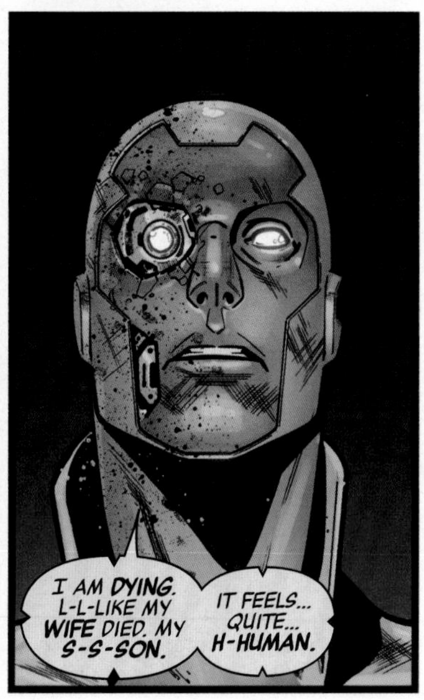
I AM DYING. L-L-LIKE MY WIFE DIED. MY S-S-SON.
IT FEELS... QUITE... H-HUMAN.

I H-H-HAVE ALL I NEED.
THANK YOU.

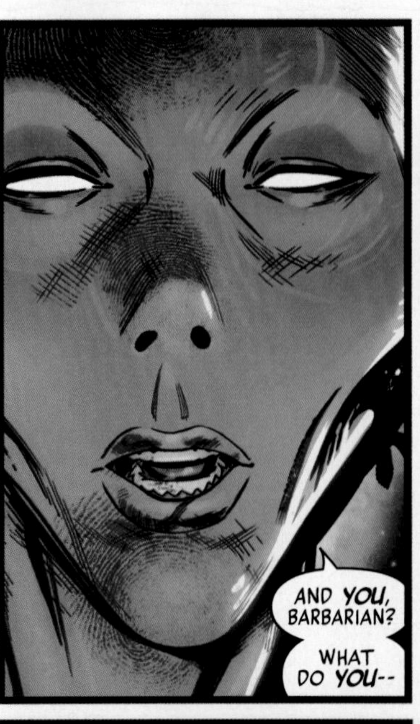
AND YOU, BARBARIAN?
WHAT DO YOU--

WAIT. WHAT DID HE SAY?
HE'S HUMAN BECAUSE HE'S DYING?

YES. ANDROIDS C-CAN BE... REBUILT.
TO BE M-M-MORTAL IS TO BE T-TR
HUMAN.

...
YOU'RE A FOOL.

YOU THINK DYING MAKES YOU HUMAN?
BEING HUMAN MAKES YOU DIE.

OUR BODIES BREAK. DISEASE CLAIMS US. DESPAIR POISONS US.
YOU THINK THA
HAS MEANIN
THAT WE WANT IT?

WE FIGHT IT!
LIKE RATS FIGHT THE TRAP!

AND WE SCREAM! AND BEG! AND CURSE! AND CROM DOES NOT CARE!
AND NEITHER DO I!
BUT WHAT I WANT-- STEEL DEVIL--

--IS FOR YO
TO FIG
BACK!

D YOU, LAST OF ALL? THE MONSTER.
TELL ME YOUR DESIRE...
...NO. NO, I WILL NOT.
I WILL NOT END YOUR WORLD.
ENOUGH THIS FOOLISH ME. YOU HAVE UR ANSWERS.
NOW GIVE ME THE SHARD OR I WILL DESTROY THIS PLANET AND SEARCH THE RUBBLE TO GET IT.
I WISH ONLY HAPPINESS AND FULFILLMENT FOR ALL.
I EVEN ALLOWED VIOLENCE TO TAKE PLACE UPON EUPHORIA SINCE SO MANY OF YOU DESIRED SUCH CONFLICT...
...BUT HARMING THE DENIZENS WHO LIVE HERE WOULD BRING PAIN AND LOSS I COULD NOT ABIDE.
HOW BEST TO PLEASE YOU AND ALL OF THEM AT THE SAME TIME?
WE'LL SEE IF YOU REMAIN DEFIANT ONCE I'VE STRIPPED ALL LIGHT FROM YOU AND SLAIN EVERY BEING WHO CALLS THIS PITIFUL SPHERE HOME.
TANG
EH?

THOK
G'YAAAAH!
ONE PERFECT SHOT, BABY!
LET'S STRIKE UP THE BAND AND MAKE SOME NOISE!
YOUR TEMERITY HAS OUTLIVED ITS AMUSEMENT, AVENGERS!
MY DARKNESS CANNOT BE OVERCOME!
MONICA, I'M PULLING LIGHT FROM ALL PROBABILITIES AROUND US AND VESTING IT WITHIN YOU!
NNNNG--!
...I-- IT'S TOO MUCH...
...I CAN'T CONTAIN IT...
YOU ARE NOT ALONE, MONICA.

WE WILL FIGHT TOGETHER...
...AND STOP THIS DARKNESS!
VISION DEALT A BLOW WORTHY OF ZEUS HIMSELF...
THE NIGHT WENCH REELS BUT IS FAR FROM SLAIN!
I'M CREATING A PATH FOR US TO PUSH THROUGH HER DARKNESS AND ATTACK, BUT WE MUST GO NOW!
NEVER!!!
WHELP, I GUESS IT'S PRIME TIME TA USE THIS LI'L BEAUTY...
YOU STOLE MY PYM PARTICLES!
YOU LITTLE--
WHO YOU CALLIN' "LITTLE"?!

THIS ROCKET IS LARGE AND IN CHARGE!
HAHAHAHAHAHAHA!
THOOM

NNNNNG!
KEEP SMASHIN'! SHE'S GOIN' DOWN!
SUCH VIOLENT MOTIVES...
...I DO NOT KNOW HOW BEST TO SERVE THEIR NEEDS.
IS THIS WHAT YOU TRULY DESIRE... DEFEAT AND DESTRUCTION?
FINAL RELEASE AFTER AN ETERNITY OF STRUGGLE?
THE NIGHT IS YOURS NO LONGER.
NO!!!
GIVE ME MY LIFE, MY POWER!
GIVE ME THE SHARD!
IF YOU MUST HAVE IT, THEN IT IS YOURS, NYX...
...TAKE IT FROM ME.

I SHALL!
KRIK
KRAK
KROOOMM

MY GODHOOD RETURNED AT LAST...
AND NOW, FINALLY, I SEE IT CLEARLY...
...THE CENTER.
THE CORE.
THE BIRTHPLACE OF ALL THAT WAS...
...ALL THAT IS...
...AND ALL THAT YET MAY BE...
FROM THIS SEAT OF POWER I SHALL REMAKE THE UNIVERSE.

...SO TIRED...CAN'T FOLLOW HER...
PLEASE, EUPHORIA...YOU NEVER HEARD... MY WISH...
VERY WELL. TELL ME, DEEP WITHIN...WHAT IS YOUR TRUE HEART'S DESIRE?
TO...
...TO BE AN AVENGER.
CHILD...ONLY ONE CAN MAKE THAT HAPPEN... AND IT IS NOT M--
...
YOU'RE RIGHT.
AVENGERS...
ASSEMBLE!

GO! GO! GO!
NYX CAN'T BE FAR AHEAD OF US, WHEREVER SHE ENDED...
...UP?

YOU GOTTA BE KIDDIN' ME!
WITH THE ENTIRE UNIVERSE TO CHOOSE FROM, NYX--THE GODDESS NYX--

LONG ISLAND
SML JKK
STRONG ISLAND
--DECIDED TO TAKE THE FIGHT TO LONG ISLAND?
I'LL DO YA TWO BETTER, TWANGY:

WHY'S THERE LIGHT COMIN' OUTTA THAT HOUSE WHEN IT'S SUPPOSED T'BE DARK ACROSS ALL CREATION--

WEIRD.
YOU HEAR SOMETHING?
WE SHOULD GET OFF THE STREET. I DON'T LIKE IT.
IT'S TOO QUIET.
--AND HOW COME NOBODY SEES IT?
OR, Y'KNOW... US?
I'M SENSING SOME SORT OF CLOAKING ENCHANTMENT. NOT FROM NYX--FROM THE HOUSE ITSELF. AS IF IT'S ACTIVELY RESISTING OUR VERY PRESENCE. IT'S--
LOOK!
NYX! SHE'S MAKING HER WAY INSIDE!
MORE FOUL SORCERY.
I AM NOT IMPRESSED, NOR W I BE BOWED! NYX WILL PA THIS NIGHT FOR HER EVILS!

SO VOWS CONAN OF CIMMERIA
CONAN!
AAAAAH!
IT'S IN MY HEAD! I CAN'T BE HERE-- THIS--IT'S HOLY GROUND!
I CAN'T BE HERE

'VE NO TIME TO MOURN LOSSES. QUICKLY, WANDA AVES A PROTECTIVE SPELL VER THOSE OF US WHO REMAIN.
IT'S ONLY DEFENSIVE. IT CAN ONLY SHIELD US, NOT ADVANCE US.

WE MUST FOLLOW NYX--
--BUT IT'S AS IF THE FORCE OF ALL CREATION WERE HOLDING FAST AGAINST US.
MY FRIENDS AND I SOLDIER FORTH, BUT EVERY STEP FEELS A THOUSAND YEARS LONG--
--AND WE ARE NOT ETERNAL, NONE OF US.
MORTALS FADE.
AS WILL I, IN TIME.

NOT
AY.
NOT BEFORE ONE LAST LABOR.
I HAVE THE DOOR!
IF I CAN KEEP IT-- HNNGH--FROM CLOSING--
--KEEP EVEN THE SMALLEST CRACKS OF LIGHT--
--IT IS STILL OPEN TO US!
SION! 'OU HEAR ME?
THE DOOR IS STILL OPEN!
I AM HERCULES, SON OF ZEUS.
I HEAR YOU, OLD FRIEND.
MONICA?
I'M GIVING YOU ALL I HAVE, VIZH--
I WAS BORN A COMBINATION OF REALITY AND MYTH-- THUS, A LEGEND. A MAN MADE OF STORIES.
BUT HERE AND NOW... IN THE FACE OF THE END...THE LEGEND FEELS HOLLOW.
I WOULD RATHER BE MYSELF.

JUST--
HURRY--
I HAVE OFTEN WONDERED WHICH OF MY MANY STORIES WILL ENDURE.
I KNOW NOW THAT THERE IS ONLY ONE THAT MATTERS:
THAT WHEN THE TIME CAME, I GAVE MY ALL...NOT TO BE THE HERO...THE LEGEND...
...BUT JUST TO HELP.
GODSPEED, VISION. FIGHT WELL.
FOR IF YOU FAIL...
...THEN ALL THE STORIES ARE DONE.

ASSEMBLY

we barrel toward the end of our weekly adventure, we wanted to give you a look at
ch things can change from the planning stage to the writing stage (and also how m
y can stay the same)! Below are the notes from our Avengers Weekly retreat early
r, blocking out the major beats in the first three issues. Though most of these ic
made the final cut, a few didn't. Can you spot which ones?.

FIRST THREE ISSUES

Character intro → Darkness falls → Voyager shows up

- Spectrum looking right at the sun, how can it be night? Adam on radio, where are you
- Hulk is going to Betty when night falls + voyager shows up
- They get to Olympus + it looks like Herc murdered everyone (Hulk attacks him?)
- Nyx shows up "You shouldn't have used my name" + blasts voyager
- Voyager gets "killed" + her dying act is to cast them to two locations
- Voyager saw fall of Olympus + saw Nyx coming out of the well
- 1st issue ends with Nyx blinding Scarlet witch
- Herc + spectrum talking about glories of godhood + living together
- Herc sent to apprehend Rocket (robbing like a radio shack) Hunting the mythic beast while telling people stories
- Spectrum wants to look vision over
- Nyx was freed by the challenger crisis, making it Voyager's problem

- ~~Spectrum wants to look vision over~~
- Spectrum "stows away" in vision by accident + pops out of Vision + punched Nyx in issue 2
- Scarlet witch blinded by Nyx at the end of 1
- Conan bit "Are you someone I know" "I doubt it." etc.

- Voyager scatters them at the end of 1
- Scarlet witch is the only mortal connected to the House of ideas
- Nightmare vision at the end of 2
- If Hawkeye's ever alone with Hulk, Hulk will kill him, end of 2 is them squaring off against each other
  - Rocket stops him from attacking + Hulk sparks nightmares
  - end 3 with hulk riding nightmare steed

you're curious to find out what secrets that line of white-out is hiding, True Believ
be sure to pick up our big finale, on sale next week! All will be revealed in the end..

10

YOU WANT TO SEE MY CREATION?

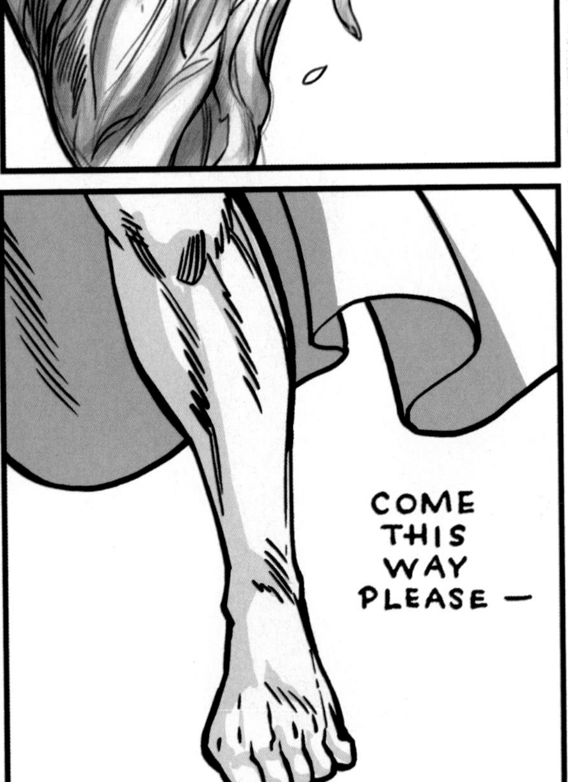

— AND I WILL SHOW YOU EVERYTHING!
0
1
I
I AM
I AM...THE VISION.

ND I AM WHOLE. CORE
EGENERATION HALTED--ALL
OGNITIVE AND PHYSICAL
FUNCTIONS RESTORED.
BUT... HOW?
THERE WAS A VOICE...
...AND I REMEMBER... A HOUSE...
THE HOUSE.
EH?
NYX, GODDESS OF NIGHT. ASCENDED NOW TO HER FULL POWER AS A PRIMAL ASPECT.
AND I AM ONLY MYSELF...
THE DWELLING SPACE OF THE FUNDAMENTAL CREATIVE FORCE OF THIS REALITY.
THE ONE ABOVE ALL OTHERS...
THE ULTIMATE FORCE OF CREATION LIVES ON LONG ISLAND?
THE HOUSE HAS MANY DOORS, AND HUMANITY HAS ALWAYS BEEN ESSENTIAL TO THE WORK.
BUT WHAT WOULD YOU KNOW OF SUCH THINGS, ANDROID?

I...HEARD A VOICE.
AN OLD VOICE...
AN ECHO FROM A TIME LONG PAST. THERE IS A NEW WORLD COMING--A NEW CREATION.
MY CREATION. REALITY REMADE IN MY IMAGE.
A COSMOS OF ETERNAL NIGHT-- AS IT SHOULD ALWAYS HAVE BEEN. BEAUTIFUL AND SILENT...
...BUT FOR THE CHIRP OF THE CRICKETS...AND SOFT BREEZES UNDER THE MOON...
YOU WOULD OVERWRITE CREATION IN CREATION'S OWN HOUSE?
SOME WOULD CALL THAT HUBRIS...
AM I NOT PLAYING OUT THE ROLE THAT WAS WRITTEN? WILL CREATION DENY WHAT IT SET IN MOTION?
NO. THERE HAVE BEEN MANY ENDINGS--THIS WILL BE ANOTHER.
YOUR WORLD OF HEROES ISN'T SPECIAL.
I DISAGREE.
AND I THINK MY ROLE HERE... IS TO SAVE IT.

YOU?
HOW CAN YOU STOP ME? HOW CAN YOU DO ANYTHING BUT WATCH?
I AM MANKIND'S FIRST DARKNESS. I AM MIDNIGHT AND MOONRISE. I AM A PRIMAL BEING, GREATER THAN GODS...
WHAT ARE YOU?
A SYNTHETIC MAN. NO MORE.
BUT...I HAVE HEARD STORIES. AND BEEN A PART OF THEM.
MY DATABASE CONTAINS THE AVENGERS FILES. A HISTORY OF EVERY HERO--EVERY MARVEL--WHO EVER FOUGHT AGAINST DARKNESS.
AND HERE...IN THIS PLACE, THIS HOUSE OF IDEAS... I FIND MYSELF WONDERING...
HOW WOULD THEY STOP YOU?

AT FIRST I THOUGHT IT ODD, A HOUSE WITH NO WINDOWS.
BUT THAT ISN'T ACCURATE.
STORIES ARE WINDOWS.
AND HERE, WHERE ALL STORIES ARE BORN, THEY ARE INFINITE IN NUMBER.
ALL ONE NEED DO TO MAKE THEM APPEAR...
...IS IMAGINE THEM.

TRICKERY.
POWER...AND POSSIBILITY.
WHAT FILLS THIS SPACE, NYX?
YOU DO NOT KNOW, FOR YOU ARE CAPABLE OF IMAGINING ONLY ONE THING:
A MULTIVERSE BUILT AROUND YOU.
THE ULTIMATE CREATION.

HARDLY.
CREATION COMES FROM LIGHT, NOT DARKNESS.
DARKNESS IS AN ENDING.
IT IS THE SHUTTERING OF IDEAS.

LIGHT IS THE BEGINNING.
THE LIGHT OF INSPIRATION.
THE LIGHT OF THE HUMAN SPIRIT.
FOREVER MIGHTIER THAN YOUR NARCISSISM, YOUR CYNICISM.
NEVER.

ALWAYS.
YOU PLANNED TO IMPOSE YOUR OWN RULES UPON OUR REALITY.
BUT THAT PLAN HAD A FUNDAMENTAL FLAW.
THIS REALITY ISN'T ABOUT RULES.
IT'S ABOUT FLYING.

IT'S ABOUT FINDING AND FANNING THE SPARK OF COURAGE IN THE DARKEST OF NIGHTS.
YOU CANNOT WIN HERE.
YOU'RE PLAYING AGAINST THE HOUSE.

THE HOUSE OF IDEAS.
THE ASTONISHING.

THE FANTASTIC.
THE AMAZING.

MARVELS.
I WAS SO CLOSE--
SO CLOSE--
THEIR FIRE, THEIR LIGHT, IS THAT OF UNFETTERED IMAGINATION--
--AND THERE IS NO DARKNESS--NOT FROM THE DAWN OF TIME TO ITS ENTROPIC END--
--THAT CAN WITHSTAND ITS GLORY!

YOU THINK YOU'VE WON, ANDROID?
THAT YOUR FIRE CAN BURN ME AWAY FOREVER?
FOOL!
I AM THE OTHER SIDE OF YOUR BRIGHT STORY!
AND I.
ALWAYS.
WILL B--
THEN I CAN ONLY PITY YOU.
BUT PERHAPS SOMEDAY, YOU WILL KNOW THE RESPLENDENCE OF THE LIGHT THAT BINDS ALL LIFE. IT WILL NOT BE EXTINGUISHED.
AND NEITHER WILL I.
NOT TODAY.

REALITY BECKONS ONCE MORE.

VISION, YOU'RE...YOU'RE ALIVE!
QUITE.
NOW, PERHAPS, MORE THAN EVER...

BEYOND
AT DOOR OF
OWER...WHAT
HAPPENED?
WHERE IS NYX?
HER DARKNESS WAS REJECTED BY THE LIGHT WITHIN.

HOLD ON.
ARE YOU SAYING
AT AN EVIL GOD
AS DEFEATED BY
A HOUSE?
NOT "A" HOUSE, CLINT.
"THE" HOUSE.

NIGHT HAS ITS PLACE IN PROPER BALANCE SET AGAINST THE LIGHT.
CORRECT.
THE DARK QUEEN MAY RETURN, BUT NOT AT THIS JUNCTURE.

IN ALL MY YEARS, I'VE NEVER FELT SUCH POWER.
WHAT DID YOU SEE IN THERE?
IT WAS, FORGIVE THE TERM, QUITE A VISION.

I SAW THE LIGHT OF PURE POSSIBILITY...

"...THE GLORIOUS ILLUMINATION WE CALL 'HOPE.'"

WE'RE BACK
TH BREAKING
NEWS--
--POWER
ESTORED ALL
OVER THE
WORLD--
-GETTING
PORTS OF
NRISE ON
HE EAST
COAST--

"--AS WELL AS FULL DAYLIGHT IN SOUTH AMERICA, AFRICA, EUROPE--
LE SOLEIL--
C'EST UN MIRACLE!

"--AND EVERYWHERE ELSE IT SHOULD BE.
"WE'LL HAVE NEWS THROUGHOUT THE DAY ON THAT--BUT PERSONALLY, THIS REPORTER WOULD LIKE TO OFFER THANKS--

TO WHICHEVER
EROES HELPED
GET THE DAY
BACK."
AVENGERS MOUNTAIN.
NO, DR. BRASHEAR-- NOT MY TEAM EITHER. BUT I SUSPECT WE'LL FIND THE AVENGERS PLAYED SOME HAND IN IT.
HOW IS YOUR END OF THINGS?
OH, YOU KNOW, T'CHALLA-- THE USUAL.

ERMANY.
NEOHEDRON AND THE TECHNOCRACY TEAMED UP TO END HUMANITY. AGAIN.
NOTHING WE CAN'T HANDLE...
BOLD WORDS, HERR BRASHEAR!
BUT MY CRYSTAL MIND FORESEES EVERY MOVE YOUR TEAM CAN--

SHHRZAKKK
OH, SHUT UP.
GAAAHHH!

...MONICA?
IN THE FLESH.
LITERALLY.

I BURNED OUT MOST OF MY POWER KEEPING VISION ALIVE AND HELPING HIM REACH... SOMEWHERE.
ANYWAY, I'M NOT SOME IMMORTAL LIGHT BEING ANYMORE.

AND...AND I WANT TO STAY THAT WAY, IF I CAN. BE HUMAN. HAVE HUMAN THINGS--A LIFE, A FAMILY.
EVEN IF...EVEN IF THAT MEANS YOU AND ME, WE'RE NOT... COMPATIBLE, OR...
HEY. HEY.

I LOVE YOU, MONICA RAMBEAU.
I'M NOT GOING TO STOP LOVING YOU. WHATEVER HAPPENS...
WE'LL WORK IT OUT.
...YEAH.

"WE'LL WORK IT OUT."
MICHIGAN.

...
HAVE YOU EVER SUFFERED?

THE RICOCHET, INTERGALACTIC DIVE BAR IN CONTINUOUS ORBIT AROUND VOORT-3.
FLUUUUUSH
WHERE'D YOU COME FROM?
ORIGINALLY, OR JUST NOW?
Y'KNOW WHAT? IT DON'T EVEN MATTER...
THAT'S RIGHT. IT DON'T.
SIGH
EVER GET TH' FEELIN' NO ONE'S GONNA APPRECIATE YAH NO MATTER WHAT YAH DO?
CONSTANTLY. IT SUCKS.
THIS WHOLE THING STARTED 'CAUSE THEY ASSUMED I WAS A THIEF.
WERE YOU?
NOT THIS TIME!
I WAS ON EARTH JUST RETURNING STUFF...PUTTIN' IT ALL BACK WHERE IT BELONGED, Y'KNOW?
THAT WAS THE PLAN... SETTLE MY DEBTS AN' GET THINGS BACK TO ZERO.
MAKE THINGS RIGHT, BEFORE...
AW, WHAT THE HELL!
HERE'S TO BEIN' AN AVENGER...
...GUESS I CAN CROSS THAT ONE OFFA MY BUCKET LIST!
HE

LOS ANGELES, CALIFORNIA.
IT'S UNFORTUNATE VOYAGER WAS UNABLE TO STAY. IT WOULD HAVE BEEN NICE TO SEE HER AGAIN.
SHE WAS NEEDED ELSEWHERE, BUT INDICATED THAT SHE WOULD TRY TO VISIT US UNDER LESS DIRE CIRCUMSTANCES IN THE FUTURE.
THAT'S THE PROBLEM WITH TELEPORTERS AND MAGIC TYPES--YOU NEVER KNOW WHEN THEY'RE GONNA POP UP AND TELL YOU EVERYTHING IS CRUMBLING... AGAIN.
SO YOU'D RATHER NOT BE WARNED ABOUT CATACLYSMIC EVIL?
IT'S FINE. JUST LEMME FINISH MY COFFEE BEFORE WE FIGHT FOR THE UNIVERSE, Y'KNOW?
HOW IS HERCULES FARING AFTER THESE TRAUMATIC EVENTS?
I BELIEVE HE RETURNED TO OLYMPUS TO MOURN THE DEAD AND GATHER SOME MEMENTOS.
IF THEY ARE INDEED DEAD...
YOU SAW OLYMPUS, VIZH. IT WAS A SLAUGHTERHOUSE.
YES.
HOWEVER, THE GODS OF OLYMPUS ARE MORE THAN JUST PHYSICAL BODIES.
THEY ARE POTENT MYTHS WOVEN INTO OUR COLLECTIVE REALITY...

"...AND I DO NOT BELIEVE THE UNIVERSE IS READY TO LET THEM GO YET."
IN A SPACE BEYOND SPACE.
KRA-KOOOMM
...THE WHEEL...HAS TURNED.
ZEUS AND HIS PEOPLE ARE BORN AGAIN.
BORN ANEW.
AND LET THE STARS TREMBLE...

THE WAY YOU SPEAK ABOUT REINCARNATION AND THE GODS, IF I DIDN'T KNOW BETTER I'D ALMOST THINK YOU'D FOUND A BIT OF FAITH, MY FRIEND.
IS IT "FAITH," JERICHO? I AM AS YET UNSURE.
I WAS PREPARED TO DIE TO FIND MY HUMANITY AND INSTEAD IT WAS FOUND THROUGH A NEED FOR LIFE.
I AM NOT "HUMAN" PER SE, BUT I NOW KNOW I AM THE CREATION OF A CREATOR AND THE END OF MY STORY HAS YET TO BE TOLD.
THAT IS SOMETHING WORTH BELIEVING IN.
ROCKET AND THE HULK DISAPPEARED, AS DID THE MAN CALLED "CONAN"...
YOU SAID THAT BARBARIAN SAVED YOUR LIFE.
YES...
HE WAS A MURDERER AND A VAGABOND, BUT HE FOLLOWED A CODE OF HONOR.
EVEN STILL, WHEREVER HE IS NOW...

"...I CERTAINLY WOULDN'T WANT TO GET IN HIS WAY."
HNNH... HNNH...
YOU THOUGHT YOURSELF WORTHY OF MY FLESH, LONG-JAW, BUT MY BITE WAS DEEPER.
NOW YOUR MEAT WILL SUSTAIN ME.
PONDER THAT WHILE YOU COOK ON MY SPIT AND SIT IN MY STOMACH.
IT FEELS GOOD TO DRIVE A STAKE INTO SOMETHING AND SEE IT DIE AS IT SHOULD.
THIS CIMMERIAN HAS HAD ENOUGH OF CURSED WITCHES, CRAZED GOLEMS AND DARK GODS FOR A LIFETIME.
I HAVE SIMPLE NEEDS.
GIVE ME SOMETHING SHARP AND , FOE TO FIND IT, AND THEN--
RRRRUMB

THE SAVAGE LAND.
HMMPH--
THAT WILL DO.

THE FAR SHORE.
UNCLE, I HAVE RETURNED!
WERE YOU WATCHING? DID YOU SEE?!
I WAS A REAL AVENGER THIS TIME, AND TOGETHER WE... WE SAVED THE UNIVERSE!
IT WAS EXHAUSTING AND GLORIOUS AND--
CHALLENGER?
...WHERE HAVE YOU GONE?

...I WAS A DEAD MAN UNTIL YOU AND YOUR PEOPLE SHOWED UP. SERIOUSLY.
I MEAN, THIS ROCK'S GOT TO BE THE HIDEOUT FOR EVERY BANDIT IN SEVEN SYSTEMS. AND I'M HERE ON MY OWN?
TALK ABOUT BEING A LONG WAY FROM HOME, AM I RIGHT?

I WOULDN'T KNOW.
EVERYWHERE'S MY HOME.
YEAH? SO, UH...NOT THAT I'M COMPLAINING AFTER YOU SAVED MY LIFE...BUT WHAT WERE YOU DOING ALL THE WAY OUT HERE?
WHAT'S YOUR STORY, BIG MAN?

IT ISN'T IMPORTANT.
WE ALL HAVE STORIES...

...AND HERCULES WOULD RATHER HEAR *YOURS*.

ou, True Believers, for making it to the end of our wonderful weekly s
king this big would have been impossible without your support, and ev
ble without the stories that came before it, including the one that start
d in the first two pages of this book is lettering from Carl Burgos' Huma
om MARVEL COMICS #1, first printed in 1939. Sometimes to write a grea
you have to look to the beginning!

ne of our goals with AVENGERS: NO ROAD HOME was to build on the character grow ercules has been experiencing in the past few years, as well as give the gods of Olymp an exciting new status quo. And what's more exciting than Greek gods in space?!

terior artist Sean Izaakse provided us incredible designs for the revitalized Zeus, the r omeland of the gods and the newly matured Hercules. Check out his design sheets belo

HERCULES WILL RETURN...

#1 VARIANT BY **MARK BROOKS**

#1-3 CONNECTING VARIANTS BY **MICO SUAYAN & RAIN BEREDO**

noto

#4-7 CONNECTING VARIANTS BY **PHIL NOTO**

#8-10 CONNECTING VARIANTS BY **MATTEO SCALERA** & **RAIN BEREDO**

#1 VARIANT BY **JUAN FERREYRA**

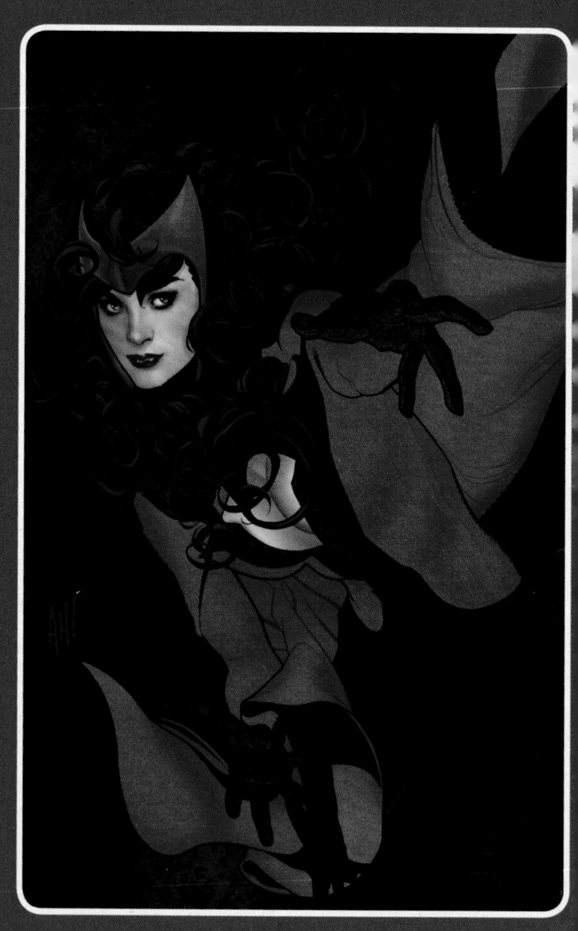

#1 VARIANT BY **ADAM HUGHES**

#6 VARIANT BY **ALEX ROSS**

#6 VARIANT BY
PATCH ZIRCHER & MORRY HOLLOWELL

#6 VARIANT BY
JIM CHEUNG & MORRY HOLLOWELL